RESPONSIBLE CAPITALISM

ESSAYS ON MORALITY, ETHICS AND BUSINESS

EDITED BY
SIR PATRICK CORMACK FSA MP
AND RUPERT GOODMAN

FIRST

LONDON • WASHINGTON

First published in the United Kingdom by FIRST, 56 Haymarket,
London SW1Y 4RN, United Kingdom, in 2009.
©2009 FIRST

FIRST is dedicated to enhancing communication between leaders in industry, finance and government, on international strategic issues. FIRST Magazine is read exclusively by this influential group of decision-makers who determine business strategies and government policy. Subscriptions are strictly limited.

All rights reserved.
No part of this publication may be reproduced, stored in a retrieval system, or transmitted in any form or by any means without the prior permission in writing of the publisher, nor be otherwise circulated in any form of binding or cover other than that in which it is published and without a similar condition including this condition being imposed on the subsequent purchaser.

ISBN: 978-0-9546409-2-7

DESIGN: HELEN EIDA
PRODUCTION: DAN HARDER
Printed in Malta

FIRST

Published by FIRST, 56 Haymarket, London SW1Y 4RN
Tel: +44 20 7389 9650   Fax: +44 20 7389 9644
Email: publisher@firstmagazine.com   URL: www.firstmagazine.com

Chairman and Founder Rupert Goodman,
Chairman, Advisory Council Rt Hon Lord Hurd of Westwell CH, CBE,
Chief Operating Officer Eamonn Daly,
Consultant, Public Affairs Sir Patrick Cormack FSA MP,
Executive Publisher & Editor Alastair Harris,
Non-Executive Directors Timothy Bunting, Hon Alexander Hambro
Award Advisory Panel, Rt Hon Lord Woolf of Barnes,
Rt Hon Lord Howe of Aberavon CH QC, Hon Philip Lader, Lord Plant of Highfield,
Chief Emeka Anyaoku GCVO TC CFR, Marilyn Carlson Nelson,
Sir Robert Wilson KCMG, Dr Daniel Vasella, Lord Marshall of Knightsbridge,
Morris Tabaksblat KBE, Ratan Tata, Howard Schultz and Philippa Foster Back OBE
Special Advisor, China, Lord Powell of Bayswater KCMG,
Special Advisor, Russia Sir Andrew Wood GCMG,
Special Advisor, Latin America Jacques Arnold,
Special Advisor, Global Issues Professor Victor Bulmer Thomas CMG OBE,
Special advisor, international Emily Kendall
New Business Advisor Amy Easterbrook
Associate Publisher Kathleen De Lacy,
Regional Publisher Declan Hartnett, **Production Manager** Helen Eida,
PA to Chairman Hilary Winstanly, **Marketing Administrator** Chris Cammack,
Editorial Consultant Jonathan Gregson, **Secretariat** Gil Pearson,
Design Consultant Stanley Glazer

ALL INFORMATION IN THIS PUBLICATION IS VERIFIED TO THE BEST OF THE AUTHORS' AND PUBLISHERS' ABILITY, BUT NO RESPONSIBILITY CAN BE ACCEPTED FOR LOSS ARISING FROM DECISIONS BASED ON THIS MATERIAL. WHERE OPINION IS EXPRESSED IT IS THAT OF THE AUTHOR.

IN MEMORY OF

RALF DAHRENDORF
LORD DAHRENDORF OF CLARE MARKET KBE FBA
1929 — 2009

SOCIOLOGIST, PHILOSOPHER, POLITICAL SCIENTIST, PARLIAMENTARIAN

CONTRIBUTORS

RUPERT GOODMAN
CHAIRMAN AND FOUNDER, FIRST

Educated at Eton and Trinity College, Cambridge, he sits on a number of corporate and international advisory boards.

SIR PATRICK CORMACK FSA MP
MEMBER OF PARLIAMENT FOR SOUTH STAFFORDSHIRE

A Member of Parliament since 1970, he has been a member of the Foreign Affairs Select Committee and a visiting fellow of St Antony's College, Oxford. He is Chairman of the Northern Ireland Affairs Committee.

THE LATE LORD DAHRENDORF KBE FBA
CHAIRMAN, FIRST AWARD ADVISORY PANEL (2000-2005)

Former Secretary of State, German Ministry of Foreign Affairs, European Commissioner for External Relations and Trade and subsequently for Research, Science and Education and then Member of the British House of Lords. He served as director of the London School of Economics and Warden of St Antony's College, Oxford. He was also a Professor of Sociology at both German and British Universities, latterly as Research Professor at the Berlin Social Research Centre.

THE RT HON THE LORD WOOLF OF BARNES FBA
CHAIRMAN, FIRST AWARD ADVISORY PANEL

Was previously a Law Lord and served as Master of the Rolls then Lord Chief Justice of England and Wales from 2000-05. He was first President of the Courts of England and Wales in 2005. He has been a non-permanent judge of the Court of Final Appeal of Hong Kong since 2003. He is president of the Qatar Civil and Commercial Court.

THE MOST REVD AND THE RT HON DR ROWAN WILLIAMS FBA
ARCHBISHOP OF CANTERBURY

Has been Archbishop of Canterbury since 2002. He previously served as Bishop of Monmouth from 1992 and Archbishop of Wales from 2000. Dr Williams is a Fellow of the British Academy and is the author of several books on theology; he is also a frequent broadcaster.

CONTRIBUTORS

PROFESSOR LORD PLANT OF HIGHFIELD
PROFESSOR OF JURISPRUDENCE AND POLITICAL PHILOSOPHY,
KING'S COLLEGE LONDON

Served as Master of St Catherine's College, Oxford from 1994-2000 and is currently a Fellow. He was previously Professor of European Political Thought at the University of Southampton.

MARILYN CARLSON NELSON
CHAIRMAN AND CHIEF EXECUTIVE OFFICER,
CARLSON COMPANIES INC

Graduated in international economics from Smith College, she leads one of the largest privately held companies in the world. The company's brands include Radisson and Regent Hotels, TGI Fridays, Carlson Marketing Group and Carlson Wagonlit Travel. She is also a director of ExxonMobil.

SIR ROBERT WILSON KCMG
CHAIRMAN, BG GROUP

Former Executive Chairman of Rio Tinto plc and has been a non-executive director of the Boots company plc, Diageo plc, BP plc and Chairman of the Economist Group. He is currently Chairman of BG Group plc and the Senior Independent Director of GlaxoSmithKline plc.

DR MOHAMED IBRAHIM
FOUNDER, MO IBRAHIM FOUNDATION AND
FOUNDER AND FORMER CHAIRMAN OF CELTEL

Set up the Mo Ibrahim Foundation in 2006 to support Great African Leadership. He is the founder and former Chairman of Celtel International one of Africa's most successful companies. He is also the founding Chairman of Satya Capital.

DR DANIEL VASELLA
CHAIRMAN AND CHIEF EXECUTIVE OFFICER, NOVARTIS AG

Also serves on the Board of Directors of PepsiCo, Inc. and the Board of Alcon. He is also a member of the International Board of Governors of the Peres Centre for Peace in Israel, the International Business Leaders Advisory Council for the Mayor of Shanghai, the Global Health Programme Advisory Panel of the Bill & Melinda Gates Foundation and is a foreign honorary member of the American Academy of Arts and Sciences.

CONTRIBUTORS

HE KAMALESH SHARMA
COMMONWEALTH SECRETARY GENERAL

Previously High Commissioner for India in London, he also served as India's permanent Representative to the United Nations and is currently Chancellor of Queen's University Belfast.

CHIEF EMEKA ANYAOKU GCVO TC CFR
PRESIDENT OF WORLD WIDE FUND FOR NATURE

Served as Nigeria's Foreign Minister and was Deputy Commonwealth Secretary General prior to serving as Commonwealth Secretary General for two terms.

THE RT HON
THE LORD HOWE OF ABERAVON CH QC
FORMER DEPUTY PRIME MINISTER, SECRETARY OF STATE FOR FOREIGN AND COMMONWEALTH AFFAIRS AND CHANCELLOR OF THE EXCHEQUER

A Cabinet Minister between 1979 and 1990, he has also served on many corporate and advisory boards.

SIR ANDREW WOOD GCMG
FORMER SENIOR DIPLOMAT AND CORPORATE ADVISOR

A member of HM Diplomatic Service from 1961-2000, latterly as Ambassador in Moscow. He has served on a number of corporate boards and has been a senior advisor to leading companies.

RATAN TATA
CHAIRMAN, TATA SONS

A Cornell graduate, he is the Chairman of India's largest conglomerate and chairs major Tata companies.

CONTENTS

FOREWORD
The moral and ethical dimensions of business
1

ONE
The genesis of the Responsible Capitalism Award
5

TWO
Wealth creation, human welfare and environmental stewardship
11

THREE
Identifying the responsible capitalist of the year
15

FOUR
Morality, ethics and trust
19

FIVE
Responsibility and capitalism
27

SIX
Can responsible capitalism survive the economic crisis?
35

SEVEN
Profit and responsibility: achieving the correct balance
43

CONTENTS *continued*

EIGHT
Responsible capitalism in conflict and post-conflict regions
49

NINE
Responsible capitalism – the continental European model
55

TEN
Responsible capitalism and the Commonwealth
61

ELEVEN
Can responsible capitalism help Africa's prosperity?
67

TWELVE
China: can capitalism continue to flourish responsibly?
75

THIRTEEN
Responsible capitalism in Russia and former Soviet countries
81

FOURTEEN
Responsible capitalism in India
87

Appendix

Index

FOREWORD

THE MORAL AND ETHICAL DIMENSIONS OF BUSINESS

RUPERT GOODMAN

GIVEN THE CURRENT ECONOMIC DOWNTURN, serious questions are being asked about the moral structure of capitalism. This compendium of essays on the role of morality, ethics, justice and trust in business highlights the need for a shift to a more responsible capitalism. This book aims to examine the challenge of ethical economic growth, the wider responsibilities of business and the importance of achieving responsible globalisation with a new more representative multilateralism.

With the growing realisation of the importance of Responsible Capitalism amongst policy makers, FIRST is proud to have initiated the Annual Award for Responsible Capitalism and delighted that it has become so widely recognised. The award was first established ten years ago in order to identify and recognise outstanding examples of business achievement that, in the words of the Award's 'guiding spirit' and former Chairman of its Judging Panel the late Lord Dahrendorf, 'transcend the tangible and the immediate and thereby contribute not just to wealth creation but to human welfare'. FIRST was created to serve as a forum for global policy makers and to promote dialogue which would lead to further international understanding and cooperation. The Award represents an important manifestation of our purpose and philosophy.

Responsible Capitalism is not about straightforward philanthropy made possible by success in business – though well-focused philanthropy is admirable in its own right. Nor is it simply the adoption of some aspects of Corporate Social Responsibility within businesses otherwise driven by profit maximisation models. Responsible Capitalism requires a fundamental integration of the needs of the wider community, care for the communities in which the business operates, environmental initiatives and support for the arts and culture, with the business's goals and processes. Above all, it is about how successful business leaders apply the principles of moral and social responsibility in the running of their business, combining social commitment with business acumen and innovation, and building a coherent philosophy in which the company's success is judged over the long-term by criteria that include sustainability, equity, and moral justice as well as standard financial benchmarks.

Against the background of a global downturn the moral aspects of competitive free markets and the globalised economy are being subjected to a thorough examination. Indeed, many would consider the conjunction of the words 'Responsible' and 'Capitalism' to be contradictory. It is not surprising that business and political leaders are calling for a new kind of ethical capitalism that is built on a broader set of values than short-term gain: that capitalism needs to operate with more responsibility and a greater regard for the moral and ethical dimensions. The question is also about achieving the right balance of responsibility between government, institutions and individuals.

From Barack Obama to Manmohan Singh, there is a growing demand for a more 'inclusive' system of generating prosperity and development. Tony Blair has called for a 'new capitalism' based on equitable values; David Cameron for a 'moral capitalism' that 'places the market within a moral framework' and 'embraces the many, not the few'. Market

FOREWORD

reform and regulation, whether it be conducted by national bodies or by multilateral institutions like the IMF or the WTO that are perhaps well suited to maintain surveillance over today's globalised and highly interactive system of capitalism, is deemed an urgent priority. Untrammelled capitalism has shown itself wanting. A new model – more ethical, more equitable, more accountable and, at the end of the day, more responsible – needs to be developed.

Many of these approaches demand the injection of values from without. The concept of Responsible Capitalism, as initiated and developed over the last decade through FIRST's Annual Awards, is that this sense of responsibility is most effective when it comes from within the organisation concerned. This volume, whose distinguished contributors survey the many different varieties of capitalism that have emerged over the past two decades – from China and Russia's versions of 'State Capitalism' to those in Africa and other developing markets – also highlights the particular challenges and constraints faced by those seeking to build a more responsible form of capitalism within different cultural and political environments. It also focuses on what it takes for a leader to combine building a world-class business while at the same time developing new ways in which to give back more to society in a focused and sustainable manner.

It was thought appropriate to mark FIRST's 25th anniversary, and the Tenth Annual Award Ceremony, with this publication. It will, we hope, be both a useful and stimulating reminder of the purpose of the Award itself. The success, and acceptance, of the Award owes much to the calibre of its Judging Panel, all of whom have given willingly, and unstintingly, of their time. Our major debt of gratitude is to the late Lord Dahrendorf, a towering figure in academic and public life for the last half century, especially in his native Germany, and in his adopted United Kingdom. His willingness to be Chairman of the Judging Panel and his development and intellectual underpinning of the concept of Responsible Capitalism was critical to the Award's acceptance, and we will always be in his debt.

Special thanks must also go to The Rt Hon The Lord Woolf of Barnes who, as Lord Chief Justice, presented the Award in 2005 and who readily agreed to succeed Lord Dahrendorf as Chairman; and to Sir Patrick Cormack who, associated with FIRST from its very beginning, introduced me to Lord Dahrendorf, and who has played a key role in nurturing the Award.

Finally I would like to thank three successive Secretaries General of the Commonwealth, Chief Emeka Anyaoku (himself a founder judge), The Rt Hon Sir Don McKinnon and His Excellency Kamalesh Sharma for all their encouragement and support and in particular, for allowing us to hold the Annual Award Ceremony in Marlborough House each year.

FIRST is particularly grateful to all who have contributed papers. These include previous award winners, judges, and presenters of the Award. The contributors provide very personal and sometimes controversial views. They have been given wide editorial latitude and we hope their thoughts and opinions will stimulate further debate about the characteristics and nature of Responsible Capitalism.

I hope you enjoy this special publication and that you will continue to support the concept of Responsible Capitalism.

CHAPTER ONE

THE GENESIS OF THE RESPONSIBLE CAPITALISM AWARD

SIR PATRICK CORMACK FSA MP

THE ANNUAL AWARD FOR Responsible Capitalism has its origins in two conversations. In 1995, as a visiting Parliamentary Fellow at St Antony's College, Oxford, I had a fascinating discussion at High Table one evening with the Warden, Lord Dahrendorf. Drawing on his vast wealth of experience in public and academic life and in international politics and commerce, he expounded not only on the importance, but the necessity, of successful capitalism, so long as it was controlled by those who took their responsibilities to the wider community seriously.

I thought of this conversation often and mentioned it to Rupert Goodman, Founder and Chairman of FIRST, at one of our regular breakfast meetings early in 1999. We had been discussing what FIRST might do to mark the new millennium. Rupert, understandably, wanted something that would further the aim of FIRST to bring about a greater degree of understanding between those who held political power, and those companies upon which the economies of all nations depend. We began to talk of initiating some sort of

RESPONSIBLE CAPITALISM

Award and, remembering my Oxford High Table conversation with Lord Dahrendorf, suggested that we might try and bring him on board. Rupert Goodman responded enthusiastically to the idea of a meeting, and Lord Dahrendorf, himself, was equally positive, when I called him later that day. So it was about three weeks later that the three of us sat down to another working breakfast.

From the beginning Ralf Dahrendorf was adamant that we were not seeking to discover influential, unknown entrepreneurs, or to reward famous ones, no matter how far they had transformed the fortunes of their companies, and even if they had been conspicuously (or better still inconspicuously) generous with the fortunes they had made.

Sadly Ralf died in June 2009, just after he had begun to prepare a piece for this publication, but his definition of Responsible Capitalism shines out from the extracts from his annual pieces for the Award programme, which follow.

On that morning in the spring of 1999 we all agreed that our mission therefore was not to acknowledge success, or even generosity, but to find those latter day Robert Owens and Titus Salts or, as Ralf put it, men, or women, who ran successful businesses, but who were always conscious, not just of their responsibilities to their work force, but to their environment and to the wider community. We were looking for business leaders whose running of their companies added value to the places where they were based, to the lives of all who lived there, and to all who consumed their products. Quality must be the hallmark of their endeavours – quality of operation and production, of service, and of delivery.

From the beginning we also agreed that our efforts would not succeed if they were perceived to have a particular agenda, or to be insular. And so we set about forming a panel of distinguished judges whose reputation would be the answer to anyone who might misconstrue our aims. At that stage Ralf sat as a Liberal Democrat in the House of Lords (two years later he moved to the Cross Benches) and so we invited two of his most respected colleagues, Lord Howe from the Conservative Benches, and Lord Plant from the Labour, to be judges. They were joined by Chief Emeka Anyaoku who was about to retire as Secretary General of the Commonwealth, and by Raymond Seitz, who had settled in London after a highly successful period as United States Ambassador here. It was agreed that I would represent the interests of FIRST. Rupert Goodman would attend all meetings, but he would not be a judge, nor cast any vote, in view of the fact that he was Chairman of the Company initiating and providing the Award.

Two further things were needed to ensure the Award had a good beginning, a suitable venue and an internationally recognised presenter for the Award itself. Chief Emeka Anyaoku provided the answer to our first question by providing Marlborough House, and Gordon Brown, then Chancellor of the Exchequer, provided the answer to the second by agreeing to make the first presentation. At the same time that we were making these arrangements, Ralf Dahrendorf was writing to Ambassadors here in London, to British Ambassadors abroad, and to other national and international figures in government, commerce and industry, inviting them to make nominations. So when the judges met for the first deliberative session early in the year 2000, some thirty five names were before us. After much deliberation, and a secret ballot, it was agreed to offer the 2000 Award to Sir John Browne, now Lord Browne of Madingley. Thus a pattern was established and Lord Woolf describes, in some detail, in his contribution, how the judges continue to operate.

From time to time we have made special awards: for lifetime achievements, for advocacy, and for the SME sector here in the UK. We are proud to have had the award accepted by business leaders from many countries, and to have had it presented by eminent leaders in public life in the UK, including Her Royal Highness, The Princess Royal, and the Archbishop of Canterbury, as well as two Foreign Secretaries and two Chancellors of the Exchequer.

RESPONSIBLE CAPITALISM

A number of those associated with the Award have contributed to these pages, and their wise words repay careful reading. After the crisis of confidence in financial institutions which has caused such economic turbulence over the last year or more, we need reassurance that those who are driving the engines of capitalism fully understand their wider responsibilities, and hold to high ideals, however hard they strive for high profit margins. Sir Robert Wilson, our second winner, and now a judge, makes a balanced and judicious assessment of the realities of challenge and reward in this context. Lord Plant of Highfield, a judge from the beginning and a leading academic, inspired by the achievements of Sir Robert and other winners, makes the observation that our winners 'have set an example to others, and in such a way that lots of myths about the incompatibility of capitalism and responsibility can be dispelled.'

The Award has acquired a truly international flavour and I am proud we have chapters from Marilyn Carlson Nelson, Dr Daniel Vasella and Ratan Tata, all winners of the Award, as well as fascinating analytical pieces on Russia, by Sir Andrew Wood, former British Ambassador in Moscow, and on China, by Lord Howe of Aberavon, himself a judge and, as Foreign Secretary, negotiator of the Hong Kong Agreement, and on Africa by Emeka Anyaoku who, before he was Commonwealth Secretary General, was Foreign Minister of Nigeria.

Perhaps the role of responsible capitalism is best summed up by Kamalesh Sharma, the current Commonwealth Secretary General, when he says, "For millions of people striving to reach their potential and to achieve greater prosperity, it remains responsible capitalism that has the greatest ability to fulfil those hopes."

It is a great disappointment to everyone who has been in any way associated with the Award that Ralf Dahrendorf did not live to contribute his chapter to this book, and to be with us at the Tenth Award Ceremony. I know just how highly he rated the Award itself and how much importance he attached to propagating the ideas of responsible capitalism. I was privileged to be able to make a brief contribution to the symposium held in his honour on May 1st 2009, his 80th birthday, at St Antony's College, Oxford. He was very frail, and had virtually lost his voice but he was on the top of his form intellectually, and he positively beamed when I mentioned our joint involvement with FIRST's Award. In his brief, but moving, reply he made plain his devotion to the causes for which he was being honoured, including this one, just as he had last year, when the Foreign Secretary presented him with his FIRST Award, a special one to acknowledge his championing of the ideals of responsible capitalism through many decades, and in many lands.

Every year while he was Chairman Ralf Dahrendorf contributed a brief, but trenchant, article to the programme, and in the next chapter we produce extracts from some of those pieces, as testimony to a great man to whom we will always owe an enormous debt for enabling us to launch this very worthwhile millennium initiative.

CHAPTER TWO

WEALTH CREATION, HUMAN WELFARE AND ENVIRONMENTAL STEWARDSHIP

QUOTES FROM LORD DAHRENDORF KBE FBA

W RITING IN THE FIRST AWARD PUBLICATION in the year 2000, Ralf began 'Capitalism is a many splendoured thing – or at least if its splendours seem tainted at times, it is multi-faceted. There are profound differences between the Italian family firm whose owners are worried about its survival for the next hundred years, the German company enveloped in structures of co-determination which promises that there will no "no redundancies for operational reasons" and the Anglo Saxon profit machine which is praised for its market value and for not offering champagne to its shareholders after the Annual General Meeting. There are other versions of the capitalist enterprise as well as mixtures of cultures. Yet they all have this in common, in that they work both in terms of their products and their profits. In other words there is not just one model of the successful modern company. The assumptions of Chicago economists and the ideals of the Harvard Business School are fine as far as they go, but reality is more varied, richer in the motives of business leaders, the culture of companies and the expectations of their environment. This is why it makes sense to offer a prize for those who practise a certain kind of capitalism; we have called it 'responsible capitalism'.

He went on, 'It is important to note that responsible capitalism is not some other type of economy. The FIRST prize is not given for adding charity to business, nor is it intended to pave the way for a non-capitalist economy. Business, charity and government – the market, civil society, and the state – each have their distinctive role to play in a liberal order. But they can play it well or badly, led by short or long term considerations, with or without regard for the wider ramifications of decisions. The prize for responsible capitalism recognises outstanding examples of business achievement which transcend the tangible and the immediate and thereby contribute not just to wealth creation but to human welfare.'

This was Lord Dahrendorf's theme throughout, not only in his writings about the Award but in the many discussions we had with him as we met for six successive years to determine on the winners under his Chairmanship.

From the beginning Lord Dahrendorf had hoped that, at a very early stage, we would be able to identify a business leader from outside Europe and the United States. In due course we succeeded, and not just once, but in 2002, ruminating on this he wrote 'Let me add the reluctant comments that in my mind at least our search raised a niggling question. Responsible Capitalism as we understand it is the combination of business success with documented involvement in issues of social development, the environment and human rights. We emphasise the combination, that is to say, it is not enough for this award at least to add philanthropic commitment to business achievement. Large profits and generous charitable giving are certainly desirable, but responsible capitalism requires the integration of commercial purposes and wider concerns. Could it be that this rare combination is more likely in mature capitalist economies than in emerging ones? Does responsible capitalism require the relative security of long standing experience in the ways of market economies embedded in democratic institutions?'

By 2003 Ralf was writing that the Award 'is becoming a recognised brand, cherished by winners'. This was the year when the Award winner was Dr Daniel Vasella of Novartis, and Ralf remarked that he 'epitomises what this Award is about. It is given to successful business leaders who in the running of their business apply principles of moral and social responsibility.' He went on 'Protecting basic human rights is the task of government. Respecting human rights is a matter of course for his company. But the company will not leave it at that. It has established guide lines of corporate citizenship which go beyond general rules or local laws in committing the company to meeting social and ecological needs.'

And once again Ralf raised a question, 'Are large companies better placed to combine profitable business with social awareness? Do they have more room for manoeuvre, possibly more people to concern themselves with ethical and moral matters? Are they more in the public eye and therefore more clearly accountable for their corporate citizenship? Or have we just simply not looked hard enough for leaders of smaller companies who would be deserving?'

In the next year, 2004, when he remarked that the Award was 'beginning to look like an institution' he provided a partial answer, at least, to the last question. Having made the point that 'what is unique about this Award. It is not an attempt to play down business success through profitable entrepreneurial activity in the name of moral values. This on the contrary is an award for outstanding examples of the possibility of combining a sense of responsibility with commercial success… …It could be called an award for sustainable capitalism.' He then went on to say that that year we had created a special award for the SME sector, looking, with the help of Members of Parliament and others throughout the UK, for candidates nearer home. That particular Award went to a couple from Norfolk who had a special approach to recruitment, flexible working and staff development... 'by offering working mothers and others mentoring and training, as well as team working and flexible scheduling they become innovators in social as well as commercial terms.' The jury considered them a model of responsible entrepreneurial success.' It was that year too, when the Award went to Morris Tabaksblat with the joint winner being Jaime Zobel de Ayala, from the Philippines. Another of Ralf's ambitions was being realised.

The last time Ralf contributed to the Award publication was in 2005. He was conscious that it was his valedictory piece because he had announced to us that he would step down from the Chair after that year's Award ceremony and Lord Woolf of Barnes had already kindly agreed to take over the Chairmanship. Ralf made the point 'This is a time when questions are asked about the moral commitment of capitalist enterprises which have served us so well in the past. People wonder about the large incomes of executives while those of lesser mortals remain steady or are declining. Questions are raised about rising profits of companies which are also laying off significant numbers of people. Is there a reversal of the relationship between growth and employment by which less employment increases growth opportunities?' He went on, 'such questions are asked and must be answered. The Responsible Capitalism Award is an answer.'

Ralf Dahrendorf was, above all else, a truly wise man. His wisdom and discernment were, I would contend, rarely seen to better effect than the way in which he nurtured this Award and guided us through its first six years.

CHAPTER THREE

IDENTIFYING THE RESPONSIBLE CAPITALIST OF THE YEAR

THE RT HON THE LORD WOOLF OF BARNES FBA

I REGARD MY INVOLVEMENT with the competition that FIRST holds annually to identify the Responsible Capitalist for the Year as extremely rewarding. I followed the late Lord Dahrendorf, who died recently, as the Chairman of the panel of judges in time to identify Ratan Tata, Chairman of the Tata Group as the winner of the 2006 competition. As one would expect of any initiative in which Lord Dahrendorf had been involved, the competition is an extremely imaginative project which had been carefully thought out and also a project to which he personally had made a very important contribution.

There are 13 judges and the experience of each means that they are uniquely qualified to assist me in identifying the candidate worthy of the award. This year there were 42 candidates drawn from all over the world. Identifying the winner is no easy task. What happens is that Ambassadors together with others whose occupation and experience makes them suitable to assist, both in this country and overseas, are invited to nominate potential award winners. This process produces a remarkable field of individuals who in different parts of the globe have made a very significant contribution to the wellbeing of society. Each candidate has obviously been a leader of a very successful company, frequently a global company. This by itself is not sufficient. More important and more difficult to assess is the extent to which their entrepreneurial skills must have also demonstrated why he or she should be regarded as being a *responsible* capitalist as well.

There are many forms which responsible capitalism can take. Obviously the business must have been conducted in a manner which is lawful. However, more than this is required. The business must also have been carried on in an ethical manner and in a way which brings real benefit to the inhabitants of the countries in which it operates.

A useful example is provided by Howard Schultz, the 2007 winner. From very modest beginnings he started and developed the Starbucks Coffee Company which now operates in a vast number of countries around the globe. His vision of the contribution that coffee houses could make to society, was not limited to the changes he made to the coffee drinking habits of his customers or even the improved working conditions of his employees, including free health care. He also improved the conditions of those, particularly the disadvantaged in Africa and especially Rwanda, who he encouraged to grow the coffee that was drunk by those frequenting his coffee houses in the more prosperous parts of the world. When he left the business it no longer flourished as it had and he had return to revitalise its operations[1].

The significance of the competition is the fact that collectively the candidates demonstrate the extraordinary contribution that successful capitalists who are *responsible* can make to society as a whole. By the time the award is given to the individual who in any particular year is felt to deserve it, his (or her) activities have made a huge impact. Often, the award winner is coming towards the end of his or her career. But this is not necessarily the case as today a remarkable contribution can be made in an extraordinarily short period of time.

Where the candidate has already devoted many years to his business,

---

[1] See The Observer Newspaper Magazine Profile 19th July 2009.

JUDGING THE COMPETITION

a problem can arise because the activities that are relied upon as demonstrating responsibility are acts of great benevolence that are funded from the massive wealth that has been accumulated in earlier years. The activities as a capitalist have provided the means by which he now exercises his philanthropy. That he does so is hugely commendable but it is not an example of what the judges regard as the responsible capitalism we are seeking. What we seek is someone who, while operating a successful business demonstrates exceptional responsibility. Nonetheless, so striking can be the scale of the benevolence that the judges do reserve the right to make a special award to mark a special contribution to society in addition to the award given to our annual award winner. We are also contemplating making an additional award to an exceptional philanthropist for a lifetime of endeavour[2].

It is most important that we can rely on those who nominate to do so with integrity and care. In the case of Ambassadors this can usually be assured. However, before making an award the credentials of the proposed winner will be carefully cross-checked.

Following the selection of the winner, the award is made at a gathering in London, usually in the splendid apartments of Marlborough House by a most distinguished figure from among those who have held the highest offices in this country in politics, the church, the law and the armed services, in addition to a member of the Royal Family[3].

The FIRST award itself is of no intrinsic value but its prestige derives from the care that is exercised in identifying the candidates, the distinction of those who are involved in the process of selecting the winner and the quality of those who have been granted the award. In addition it is fortunate that those who initially were responsible for establishing the award have been associated with it throughout its life and have been its devoted guardians. They are Sir Patrick Cormack MP and Rupert Goodman.

At the time when the FIRST award was established the recent financial crisis could not have been foreseen but it has undoubtedly

---

[2] *In 2008, Sir Sigmund Sternberg and Lord Dahrendorf received special awards.*
[3] *HRH The Princess Royal presented the award in 2006.*

increased its significance. Capitalism as a whole has been tarnished. It is most important that the events which caused the crisis should be seen in context. At the same time as recklessness was occurring in some large financial institutions, causing great hardship and havoc to large sections of the population, other institutions, out of the media headlines, were continuing to operate responsibly to improve the position of those who benefited from their activities.

It is because corporations and in particular global companies can have either a negative or positive impact on society that it is so important that responsible capitalism is promoted. This is what in its modest way the FIRST award does. It draws attention to the remarkable activities of those who are committed to conducting business in a way which is demonstrably responsible. They are sensitive to the environmental consequences of their activities. They realise the importance of conducting their business in a way which benefits others in society. Usually their experience from doing this is that their business flourishes more than if they had less regard for the wellbeing of their fellow citizens.

Each year there is only one award winner but it is my belief that the competition produces beneficial results for many. In a sense it makes us all winners. The award winners set the standards which we hope others will follow.

CHAPTER FOUR

MORALITY, ETHICS AND TRUST

MOST REV AND THE RT HON DR ROWAN WILLIAMS FBA

Has there been a crisis in the moral structure of unregulated capitalism? Does the free market mechanism fail to impute value to such concepts as morality, ethics, justice and trust?

It is interesting to note that if one reviews the literature over the past five or six years there have been a number of people inside the global economic world suggesting that a moral crisis exists in our economic system and that we have lost our compass, we have no clear sense of how trust is to be built and sustained and no clear sense of long term purpose. For example, John Dunning[1] wrote some six years ago about what he termed 'the crisis in the moral ecology of unregulated capitalism' and he along with other contributors discussed how 'circles of failure' could be created in the global economy as a consequence of moral indifference, institutional crisis and market failure. So I think there has been recognition that there exists a moral vacuum in unregulated capitalism.

The second part of your question revolves around the ability of the market to value conceptual issues such as morality, ethics, justice, trust and so on. The market mechanism takes it for granted that the central governing definition of worth or value is exchange value, not

---

[1] *'Making Globalisation Good'*, 2003

value in human growth overall, to environmental security and other things, but what can be traded, what can be exchanged. This is a good question to ask and I think that in recent years economists, business leaders and others, have been factoring in more and more elements of what the market ought to mean and it suggests an awareness of the inadequacy of this economic model. So, for example, some have underlined the importance of accounting for environmental cost as part of broader market calculations – this is a clear demonstration to me of the growing awareness that something is wrong with a one dimensional focus on the market mechanism.

Has the definition of what is ethical and moral changed? Has moral indifference contributed to the financial crisis?

This is a big question. I do not think that the definitions have actually changed. I think that there has been a rather heavy price paid for concentrating on functional and procedural efficiency and effectiveness as opposed to focusing on questions about the long-term growth of business within society and therefore the goals of society itself.

I think the effect of this has been to erode people's sense of the importance of human character – this is a very Victorian thing to say in one sense, but why not? What you might call the classical business ethic has a lot to do with character, a lot to do with dependability, with diligence, with transparency and these have not been virtues very much to the fore in the rather overheated atmosphere over the recent period.

So business and financial leaders must question their overemphasis on short-termism – any business operation that depends on profit maximisation at maximum speed must also focus on other considerations. There needs to be a recognition that an ethical modus operandi is based on trust and the trustworthiness of the participants – 'my word is my bond' is the bottom line for all transactions – and that a viable business ethic involves awareness of the long-term effect on society and the environment of any business decision.

We also need to question the purpose of economic growth – what is the purpose of profit in the wider social context? I am not suggesting that business exists simply to serve a social function – that would be an odd even a constraining remit – but when business loses sight of the overall social good, something inevitably goes wrong. If business ends up with a flat, one dimensional focus on exchange value and no sense of what is being contributed for the social good, difficulties will inevitably ensue.

You have talked about the importance of the 'social good' in an ethical business model but most business transactions involve the gain of 'competitive advantage'. How does one balance these potentially competing concepts?

Let me clarify this point. I have suggested that the concept of ethics itself is central to human life, in which the needs of others are allowed to shape our own actions and decisions.

I recognise that in day-to-day business practice, since businesses are not charities, they cannot take full responsibility for the disadvantaged but by placing business enterprises within the wider social setting, it is legitimate to analyse the extent to which they are serving the human good and meeting human needs which are not just frivolous ones. Business is a common enterprise with a responsibility both to employees, shareholders and customers and part of its moral focus must be about doing the right thing by those contracts and promises. Once a business enterprise has satisfied those obligations it is right that questions should be asked about the moral direction of the business and where it fits into society. It is also important in this regard to make the distinction between the responsibility of business and sheer charitable giving.

Most economic models are based on the concept of 'economic rational man' and the mechanisms of generating money (or profit). Does there need to be a shift towards a more 'responsible capitalism'?

It is interesting again to review the historical literature. Almost exactly one hundred years ago, Christian economic commentators were questioning the concept of 'homo economicus' where human decisions are made on rational economic grounds. The fact is, of course, that even within economic transactions people do not always behave rationally in the sense of seeking maximum self-interest and that in itself predisposes the definition of what is rational that leaves out the wider obligations and affiliations that we have. In this context I have been much influenced by the work of Sergei Bulgakov, the Russian Orthodox writer who was originally a professional economist and who became a theologian and Priest, who suggested the importance of binding together economics, creativity and contemplation[2]. I think this is a key point in today's world.

To what extent should business leaders account for the environmental costs and liabilities created by their business activities?

I have often quoted the slogan 'human economy is a wholly owned subsidiary of the environment'. It is clear that there are actual limits to material growth prescribed by our environment and that our resources are finite. Therefore one has to factor in a long-term value to these environmental resources which provide both material benefits as well as being a source of human delight, enjoyment and refreshment.

The critical question is then if we are incapable of self-regulation in this area then governments must play a role. However, no one national government can resolve these challenges alone and if there were to be legislatory provision it would have to be universally enforceable which is almost unimaginable.

There are a number of strategies that can be deployed. For example if China and India are to develop as heavily polluting economies this will be at everybody's cost – it is everyone's business not just a local problem. On the one hand we can pursue a 'licence to pollute' model, the trading of licences and the taxation of pollution on a global scale or we can pursue an intensive investment model. The latter course depends on the extent to which those developed economies are prepared to

---

[2] *The Philosophy of Economy, 1912*

finance this investment since we cannot simply sit back.

In addition the developing world wants the opportunity to develop further and is not terribly impressed by the fact that we, in the industrial world, have belatedly woken up to a morality which we are now trying to sell to the rest of the world.

I fully understand why China, in particular, feels hard done by. In my visits to China, it is very clear that their leaders are very aware of the environmental issues in both local and national governmental circles. I recently met a very interesting group of young people in Shanghai who wanted to discuss the ethics of environmental care and even the religious perspective on this issue, which was wonderful. So there is certainly a willingness to address these critical questions.

How would you define ethical economic growth – what are the ingredients and characteristics?

Again this is an important and wide-ranging question and it is interesting to consider what the economy would look like if it wasn't wholly growth-orientated.

The notion of indefinite material growth as an intelligible goal doesn't seem to me to make much sense. 'Ethical Growth', as I understand it, would be a situation where access to the market is secured where the profits of one's labour are not wholly divorced from one's own control and one's local environment and where there is sufficient surplus in the economy to meet the needs of people who are not economically productive including the very old, the very young, the vulnerable, and the disabled.

I believe that if these ingredients are put together one begins to see what the goals of economic growth might be in human terms, not simply arithmetic ones – ethical growth as you have called it.

You have talked about an obligation of an 'ethical economy' to meet the needs of the vulnerable. Do you believe that business has a responsibility for the wider community – perhaps including the provision of medical facilities, schools and so forth – areas which are traditionally the domain of government?

In the last decade, or so, we have moved away from the simple assumption that government alone carries the burden of social provision. We have moved into an era where it is taken for granted that business partnership is a good thing, although I have one or two questions about how it's worked out here and there especially in the educational world and I imagine the prison service. I do, however, think there is an ethical case for these partnership models that is not merely a simple way of government divesting responsibility for activities they ought to be shouldering but a clear demonstration that the financing of a sustainable welfare environment is a proper use of business profit.

Businesses represent both a contribution to, and a claim on, the community – businesses can be a drain on community facilities as well as an important factor in sustaining them. I think business managers do now acknowledge and recognise that their operations in a particular location bring a measure of obligation. This issue is not necessarily just about altruism – looking at the question of business responsibility for the community on a wider front, one can also frame it as a long range self-interest question and not just an abstractly ethical one.

Do international organisations such as the WTO and G20 have a role to play in encouraging and promoting a new, more responsible globalisation and a new, more representative multilateralism?

I certainly think this to be the case. As we have discussed earlier virtually all of the economic problems we face are insoluble by any one country acting alone and we have got to move beyond a world of competing trade alliances towards a world in which at least some global agencies are able to act as trusted global brokers – people who can look at the imbalances that arise between economies and not in a global sense sort them out but at least keep the issues alive for governments and help maintain a long-term perspective.

It is clear to me that some of our global and national economic problems are the result of certain weaknesses in some of these global institutions. I would like to think that the Church would be among those institutions which could be trusted to act as a global broker.

What is your vision for the role of faith and spirituality as a guide through the global economic crisis?

I think many people now freely acknowledge that there exists a spiritual void in terms of relationships and trust and this brings me to the central contribution that any religion can bring to this debate and that is a sense of the richness of the human, of the Christian, made in the image of God and that is an image of creativity, liberty and interdependence. The fundamental issue, I think, is not simply what we want to know about God and our responsibility before God, important as that is, it is also our responsibility to be human and to encourage the interdependence of people.

Dr Rowan Williams was in conversation with Rupert Goodman.

CHAPTER FIVE

RESPONSIBILITY AND CAPITALISM

LORD PLANT OF HIGHFIELD

What is the moral responsibility of the firm or the individual in a capitalist economy? How wide is the scope of any such responsibility and what role if any should government have in enforcing the recognition and the discharge of any such responsibilities? These issues are very salient at the moment in the context of the international financial crisis because many claim that at the roots of the crisis lie both a failure to act responsibly on the part of financial institutions and a failure of government to regulate effectively and to enforce appropriate standards of responsible behaviour. Although to be sure these issues are at the forefront of present debates nevertheless the relationship between capitalism and morality has a very long history and some aspects of that history are still instructive.

It is frequently remarked that while it is true that Adam Smith wrote his *Enquiry into the Causes of the Wealth of Nations*, which has assumed canonical status as a basic text for the theory of the capitalist market economy, he also wrote *A Theory of the Moral Sentiments* which led him to see that market behaviour has to have an intrinsic moral dimension. Indeed some thinkers have argued that a set of prevailing moral and religious ideas were in fact crucial for the emergence of the capitalist economy. Max Weber argued in *The Protestant Ethic and the Spirit of Capitalism* that the development of Calvinist Christianity was an essential precondition for the creation of capitalism. The crucial reason was that it provided the conditions necessary for capital accumulation. Given the rather terrifying doctrine of predestination it was held by Calvinistic and other puritan moralists that while one could not earn one's salvation, nevertheless, success in a worldly calling could be regarded as a sign that one was predestined to salvation since such success indicated God's favour. So the pursuit of success had a religious dimension, as it still has for many Protestants in the USA. However, in Weber's view such pursuit of success was also linked to draconian constraints on consumption – puritan morality restricted personal consumption and so the combination of seeking success and constraints on consumption led to the accumulation of capital, a precondition for the development of the capitalist economy. The point, which is still relevant for today is that capitalism depended upon a moral framework which provided an environment of responsibility in the pursuit of success. It also provided the moral basis for the sanctity of contracts, for trust, for truth telling and for the kind of ethos in which 'my word is my bond' made sense. One way of putting the point is that the moral basis of capitalism provided a sense of civic virtue within capitalism.

Today the situation is very different. We still need trust, confidence in contracts, responsibility and some sense of the constraints on self interested behaviour and while we still need these the Judaeo Christian basis on which they rested has become eroded. This tradition provided a moral heritage which has now been eroded by the decline in religious belief associated with secularisation which has itself been closely allied to capitalism. This has been pointed out by a large number of thinkers ranging from Karl Marx, Karl Polanyi, Schumpeter and more recently Francis Fukuyama. The argument is also put in terms of social capital. The idea is that capitalism needs social capital and that trust, cooperation, responsibility, truth telling and the like constitute part of the social capital without which capitalism cannot thrive. No doubt it depends on human capital: skills, ingenuity, entrepreneurship, innovation and so forth; it also depends on finance capital on the financial resources necessary for investment. Nevertheless it will not thrive without social capital.

In the view of some thinkers, one of the factors which has exacerbated the detachment of capitalism from a moral basis has been the growing divorce between the ownership and control of firms. In the 19th Century, in many ways the heyday of capitalism, the typical firm was owned by an individual, a family or perhaps a small group of like-minded people who took their duties of ownership seriously. We may now deplore many of the effects of this in terms of the exploitation of employees and the environment – although there were notable exceptions to this in two respects. In the first place some owning families, for example the Rowntrees and the Cadburys, no doubt as the result of their religious beliefs sought to run their firms in terms of what they saw as important moral values; others sought to run their firms in pretty ruthless ways and yet used their profits to encourage the arts, sciences, the Victorian universities and by helping to finance civic building and the like, giving them a sense of civic pride and responsibility. So owners could seek to act according to a moral code within their enterprises or they could use their profits in the pursuit of civic virtue broadly conceived. This sort of ownership meant that there was no gap of accountability within the firm. Those who managed the firm knew that they had to manage it according to the priorities of the owners.

However, with the advent of what James Burnham in a famous book called the 'managerial revolution', there has been a divide between ownership and control. The major agent of this change was the widening and dispersing of share ownership so that instead of firms being owned by individuals, families or a group of the like-minded, ownership has now been dispersed amongst potentially many thousands of share holders. This has led to a gap in accountability and, it is argued, it is no longer clear to whom managers are responsible and what should be the imperatives which should guide their actions. One answer, prevalent in the 1980s and 1990s, was that the only imperative on a firm was to return ever-increasing value to the shareholders. This value had to be seen in monetary terms and this may well have acted as a further erosion of the kind of ethical context characteristic of earlier versions of capitalism. Neither ethical goals within the firm nor external concerns which, as I have said, were a concern of 19th century industrialists are easily compatible with returning increasing value to the shareholder. This is exacerbated by the inability of shareholders to exercise much control over the priorities of boards of directors. This has been shown recently in respect of the banks. There are two aspects of this. The first is that the firm – whether a bank or an industrial firm – has a very strong incentive to keep autonomy in management and to pursue its own agenda in terms of returning shareholder value and the assumption is that shareholders will not much care what this agenda is so long as it does return such value. Secondly the very complexity of the products produced by the firm may well outrun any capacity of the shareholders or their representatives to hold the directors and managers to account. This is particularly true in the case of the banks, where things like securitised debt obligations and complex swap arrangements, were agreed to even by directors who had little or no idea what these complex products actually were, never mind the shareholders.

The problem of the accountability of managers has been made more complex because even the imperative to return value to shareholders has under pressure had to be set in a context in which other concerns play a role. This is most notably true of the environmental impact of the business concerned. It is of course true that, since the advent of trades unions, managers have had to be concerned about a wider set of interests rather than just shareholders. Nevertheless there are differences between union influences and factors like the environment. The main one, of course, is that the environment is of general concern whether one is a shareholder, consumer, manager, employee or a member of the general public. The problem for managers is how to incorporate such concerns within a firm which sees its main task as being that of returning shareholder value. Of course there are ways of trying to secure this by regulation or by legal requirements, whether in the civil or the criminal courts, that the polluter is responsible for the environmental impact of the firm's activities. This will alter the costs of production and it may well turn out that the best way to return shareholder value is to comply with regulations since the costs of non-compliance, either in financial or reputational terms, of both may well have an effect on the profitability of the firm. The important point here though is that government has had to step in with regulation since the country at large cannot rely on managers or boards to behave in a responsible manner without the constraints in regulation being taken into account.

There is a dilemma here which goes to the heart of the issue of morality and capitalism. As I said earlier there is a need for some kind of civic virtue or, in more modern parlance, a degree of social capital if capitalism is to work in an acceptable way. At the same time however there is a very strong incentive for any individual to evade this. To illustrate the point at stake here let us take the case of monopoly. It is central to the coherence of the idea of free market capitalism that monopoly is a bad thing. Competition spurs innovation, entrepreneurship and is essential to the price mechanism. In a sense competition is a kind of civic good within the economy and monopoly is a civic bad. However, when one looks at the individual business decision maker he (or she) has every incentive to pursue monopoly for his (or her) product because prices can be increased and profits enhanced. Why should this person be concerned with what is in the interests of the market economy overall, that is to say the avoidance of monopoly? What concern is civic virtue to him or her if profit can be increased by disregarding this?

One answer that might be given is that it is in everyone's long-term interest to avoid monopoly and this applies to this business man as much as anyone else. But, it might be argued, why should he or she take a longer term view. After all as Lord Keynes said: "In the long term we are all dead." Given the decline in religious belief and growing moral pluralism and subjectivism it becomes very difficult to set out a compelling case at the individual level for the longer term view. This, it might be argued, is true of shareholders as much as managers because in the long run they are all dead as well. Constraints on consumption and on anti-competitive behaviour becomes more difficult in the context of a desire for instant gratification.

Given that it is difficult to see a solution to this problem other than government regulation against behaviour which will damage the interests of the market as a whole then are we in a position where we have to say that government has to step in with law and regulation to remedy the lack of a moral ethos in the market? This might be done in several ways. The first, of course, is to strengthen regulatory frameworks to constrain behaviour which will not be self-controlled whether it is in terms of over exuberant risk-taking, the seeking of bonuses, even when not matched by performance, which may in turn strengthen over exuberance. It might be done by regulation or by tax regimes to wean firms and shareholders off short-termism. It might also be done in the way suggested recently by Lord Myners by strengthening the role of shareholders and giving them a sense of ownership of companies by altering voting rights for example. This would, as he sees it, limit the effect on companies' behaviour of a lack of involved ownership.

The problem is, that whether government acts via law and regulation or by strengthening the rights of ownership, we cannot get away from the need for some sense of moral responsibility whether at the individual or corporate level. After all, any set of laws or regulations has to achieve some degree of democratic consent which means that what is supposed to be regulated must be regarded as unreasonable. Government cannot legislate in a vacuum. It has to draw, to some extent at least, on an assumed set of views about what is reasonable and unreasonable behaviour. So regulation cannot avoid the problem of what I have called civic virtue in capitalism. The same is also true in terms of trying to close the gap between ownership and control. It may be a very good idea to increase the sense of ownership by shareholders but there is no guarantee at all that they will exercise this control in a way as to avoid unreasonable behaviour by the firm. They may be equally short-termist and concerned with instant gratification as much as anyone else. Indeed if we are to believe what the City argued in the 80s and 90s about the overriding imperative of shareholder value we have every reason to think that they will be. This would not seem to avoid the need for regulation unless there was to be a substantial change in the attitudes of shareholders, even if it is assumed that they would be prepared to take on the duties of being real owners of companies. Also it is not at all clear that in the area of finance that shareholders will be able to exert any more control over both exotic (and often toxic) assets than boards of directors are.

One thing that can be done, however, and this brings me to the FIRST Award for Responsible Capitalism is to recognise and celebrate companies which are successful, can take a long term view, and do return value to shareholders. It is too easy both for defenders and critics of capitalism to assume that profit and responsibility are in conflict with one another. The history of the FIRST Award shows that this is not so. I have stressed the importance of some moral sense to capitalism if it is to survive. One way of getting people to behave reasonably and responsibly in every day life is at the micro level of personal example. The FIRST Award winners have set an example to others and in such a way that lots of myths about the incompatibility of capitalism and responsibility can be dispelled.

CHAPTER SIX

CAN RESPONSIBLE CAPITALISM SURVIVE THE ECONOMIC CRISIS?

MARILYN CARLSON NELSON

THE QUESTION – can responsible capitalism survive current global economic challenges – is one certainly on the minds of good-thinking businesspeople everywhere these days. However, as earnest and well-intentioned as it is, the question itself has roots in a fallacy that must be rejected: that 'responsible capitalism' somehow stands apart from corporate success.

Instead, we should turn the question on its head, and ask "can any business practise irresponsible capitalism and expect to survive this or any future economic crisis?"

I have found that discussing 'responsible capitalism' as anything other than a deeply integral element of modern business reduces it to the level of an expendable luxury – something that should and can be reduced or jettisoned in challenging times, akin to first-class air travel or corporate seats at the opera house.

Thankfully, most enduringly successful leaders of corporations have come to the understanding that they are but temporary stewards of great enterprises, and have abandoned such anachronistic notions. One may as well propose to such leaders that they reduce their company's environmental safeguards in order to weather an economic storm, or that they cease critical maintenance of machinery to bolster that quarter's bottom line. They would reject such short-sighted notions, as would their boards and shareholders.

By accepting the CEO role, leaders pledge themselves to add, rather than extract, value. They understand their role and thereby protect and grow a corporate asset which, once lost, would be costly or sometimes impossible to recover.

According to Charles Fombrun, executive director of The Reputation Institute and former Professor at New York University's Stern School of Business "It can be proven that a 5% change in a company's reputation can equal a 1-5% change in its market value; and that companies with high reputations weather economic storms far better than those with low or no reputation." Further, Fombrun has found most companies that do not succeed have typically undervalued their marketplace reputation.

What is marketplace reputation, other than a by-product of doing business responsibly? Why would any business leader choose to do otherwise? Recently, I came across two interesting perspectives on the question. One, put forth by author and prize-winning journalist David Lebedoff, suggests that a disappearance of 'shared morality' is to blame for a decline in responsible actions in society. In a secular world, he posits, fewer people believe in basic concepts of what is right and what is good. They believe even less in the eternal nature of the spirit, in any form. It follows, then, that without any transcendent beliefs to guide them, decisions are routinely made almost exclusively on the immediate and empirical and with little or any consideration of the common good. Lebedoff suggests that without a belief in heaven or hell, there is no desire to follow heavenly precepts on this mortal coil. (Or to fear creating hell in our midst.)

New York Times Op-Ed columnist David Brooks, addresses the topic from a cultural rather than religious perspective. In a column published in the International Herald Tribune during the Beijing Olympics, he noted that Western cultures have tended to draw their values from ancient Greece, with an emphasis on individual heroism, while other cultures have emanated from more tribal, or "collective" philosophies.

Brooks maintains there are relatively few individualistic societies on earth, and that the Olympic opening ceremonies served as a living metaphor for the concept of collectivism – a high-tech vision of the "harmonious society" that has fuelled China's miraculous growth. He concludes by saying that China may be proving that the ideal of a "harmonious collective" may turn out to be as attractive for our times as the "individual dream."

Might this truly be an era when collective thinking is on the rise? If so, it may be incumbent upon those of us in individualistic societies to espouse a "Declaration of Interdependence." Acknowledging such interdependence need not be antithetical to individual achievement, which has long been the heart and soul of capitalism and free markets. Without a doubt, the free market has been the driver of progress for all of humankind. Neither is there a doubt that we have come to a point in human history where the free market demands a non-negotiable appreciation for the common good from its practitioners: a "shared morality" which is at the centre of responsible capitalism. In our global, interconnected age, one might make the mistake of believing that a common morality would be easier to share than ever before. One would be mistaken.

Among the greatest casualties of the connected age has been a "common" anything. Almost infinite choices can be had in everything from goods to information to truth. Yes, in the connected age, enough versions of "truth" are available that each person can choose their own. Unbelievably, there is a champion somewhere for every decision however imprudent, irresponsible or immoral. The concept of "common morality" is clearly more uncommon than ever before.

In such an age, it has become more critical than ever that corrective action be taken. Politicians may discuss and debate the need for more rules and regulations, but realists know that no amount of laws can wholly legislate collective or individual morality. The 'correction' must also be at a deeply personal level, within each of us.

The challenge, as so often has happened throughout history, has been taken up by the young. Witness the creation and propagation of 'honour oaths' at prestigious graduate schools of business. The first was The Thunderbird School of Global Management Oath of Honor (www.thunderbird.edu), established at the school in 2004. Thunderbird's Oath was created by the student-run Thunderbird Honor Council when school president Ángel Cabrera challenged students to become the first business school with such an oath – a set of principles that would guide students during their post-education careers in business.

The students responded by drafting a set of guidelines deriving from the school's belief that "global managers must contribute to the creation of sustainable economic and social value." Its followers promise:

As a Thunderbird and a global citizen, I promise:
I will strive to act with honesty and integrity,
I will respect the rights and dignity of all people,
I will strive to create sustainable prosperity worldwide,
I will oppose all forms of corruption and exploitation, and
I will take responsibility for my actions.
As I hold true to these principles, it is my hope that I may enjoy an honorable reputation and peace of conscience.
This pledge I make freely and upon my honor.

Or, consider the Harvard Business School's MBA Oath (www.mbaoath.com), begun this year by 33 HBS students with a hope of improving B-school ethics. The oath's preamble states that *"As a manager, my purpose is to serve the greater good by bringing people and resources together to create value that no single individual can create alone. Therefore I will seek a course that enhances the value my enterprise can create for society over the long term. I recognise my decisions can have far-reaching consequences that affect the well-being of individuals inside and outside my enterprise, today and in the future."*

The authors of the Harvard oath hoped they would get 100 classmates to commit to it – instead more than 50% of this year's graduating class signed on. Even more encouraging: such commitments by the business leaders of tomorrow are going viral, and global. The Harvard MBA Oath website has attracted visitors from 115 countries representing 49 languages, and the concept of an oath has already spread to Northwestern University's Kellogg School of Management and Oxford University's Saïd Business School. There are plans for translation of the HBS oath into German, French, and Spanish due to the many requests received.

Similarly, the Thunderbird Oath has been featured repeatedly on national radio, in *Time Magazine*'s recent cover story on "The Future of Work," and at many academic, business and government conferences, including the United Nations Global Compact.

In the end, student oaths – however promising – are mostly about tomorrow. To paraphrase the saying, "that will be then, what about now?" The Greeks told us that "a people are known by the heroes they crown." I believe, like them, that we must hold high those in our midst who we deem heroes – companies doing business today already operating according to established socially responsible and sustainable tenets. With modesty I consider my own company one among so many others, including corporations small, large, and even the largest. It is my honour to serve on the board of ExxonMobil, and as a board member I am familiar with the expectation of adherence to the company's ethics policy by directors, executives and employees.

An important codicil in that policy makes clear that "even where the law is permissive, the Corporation chooses the course of highest integrity. Local customs, traditions, and mores differ from place to place… but honesty is not criticised in any culture…" ExxonMobil believes that "a well-founded reputation for scrupulous dealing is in itself a priceless corporate asset."

RESPONSIBLE CAPITALISM

The company further underscores its core belief in responsible business with the admonition that "the Corporation cares *how* results are obtained, not just that they *are* obtained."

There is no doubt that the great majority of companies operate according to established – if not codified – standards. As a percentage, it is but a micro-percentage that conducts themselves without regard for the good of the many. It is up to those of us who choose to act responsibly to make clear that the vast majority of capitalists are, at the same time socially responsible. Only in this way will we reverse a wildly inaccurate accounting of all business as inherently bad.

Since the dawn of our new century, Lord Dahrendorf and FIRST have been engaged in this important work. They have honoured those companies and leaders who have distinguished themselves by their conduct, and in doing so, defining for us all the very concept of responsible capitalism. For this we owe them our deepest thanks.

Though my own company – CARLSON – is a family-held enterprise, and as such faces different pressures and challenges than publicly held companies, just as important to us is the defining of common truths and the creation of a shared morality that will help guide future generations of leaders (In our case, family members). In a personal attempt to create a shared morality concerning how our business should be conducted, a few years ago I penned a letter of guidance to our "future shareholders." To my children, grandchildren, nephews, nieces and family members to follow:

My purpose in writing this is to lay down for you what I believe are important truths about business and leadership. I am, as you will someday be, a living link between the past and the future. The ultimate measure of my success as a leader will be whether or not our company continues to prosper and thrive long after I am gone.

It has been written that "the true value of a business leader cannot be judged until he or she has been gone at least ten years – only then can the world determine whether that person's leadership was sound. This is the ultimate question which must be answered: Will the world say a company served as a positive link between the past and the future of their communities; that it added value, and helped society prosper?

The long-term sustainability and success of any business, or society for that matter, has everything to do with the ability of its leadership to think and act beyond the horizon of the current generation.

The world will always face problems. The question I hope you will ask yourself is, "What might I do to be part of the solution? What actions must I take to promote understanding, be more inclusive, show more leadership? You must always remember that you are a link in the chain. You do not exist in a vacuum. The actions you will take today will influence those who follow you, just as certainly as the actions Curt (Carlson) took to found our family's company in 1938 are influencing your life today.

For many years it has been my pleasure and honour to know and admire Lord Dahrendorf and his associates Sir Patrick Cormack and Rupert Goodman at FIRST, who have long believed in the necessity of intertwining responsible and sustainable capitalism. We are all indebted to them for showing that such a thing is important and possible, and for their important work of crowning the heroes who exist in our midst.

CHAPTER SEVEN

PROFIT AND RESPONSIBILITY: ACHIEVING THE CORRECT BALANCE

SIR ROBERT WILSON KCMG

IN AGREEING TO WRITE A PIECE under this title, my initial reaction was that it was based on a false premise: namely, that profit and responsibility are the components of a zero-sum game – i.e. that more profit necessarily means less responsibility and, conversely, that responsibility can only be borne at the expense of profit foregone. This, I believe, is fundamentally wrong.

In contrast, I would argue that profit and responsibility are both essential to long-term business success. Without profit, a company cannot grow and, ultimately, will not survive. Without responsibility, few companies are able to attract and retain the customer loyalty, high calibre employees or the other long-term relationships which are the pre-conditions for long-term business success. Profit and responsibility are interdependent constituents in a successful company.

I think that a large majority of the leaders of major companies would broadly agree with my position, but I have to admit that it is an oversimplification. It does not begin to explain the undoubted success of some of the asset strippers and corporate raiders of recent decades unless, perhaps, we have different concepts of responsibility.

Herein lies a real issue. Many free-market economists, business school academics and commentators have argued that the duty of business should be to maximise profits, subject only to the constraints of the law. They maintain that it is up to legislators to determine the framework within which business can operate and responsible leaders of public companies should seek to maximise corporate value within those constraints. The argument is extended by some to say that business leaders who shackle themselves with additional requirements are being self-indulgent at the expense of their shareholders.

On the face of it, the views of free-market theorists are irreconcilable with the strongly-held opinions of very many corporate leaders. Here, though, I refer back to my injection of the words long-term in qualifying business success. A short-term profit-maximiser may need to do no more than comply with the law, but in order to create long-term profit it is, in my opinion, necessary to work within a wider value framework.

My career experience has been predominantly in the extractive industries – most of my career as an executive in the mining industry with Rio Tinto and more recently as Chairman of BG Group. Whether mining or oil and gas, the extractive industries are characterised by long lead-times and are highly capital intensive. The raw materials produced are the essential pillars of modern economic life, but the extractive processes have environmental implications and sometimes involve sensitive community relations issues and challenges. Of course there are some companies in extractive industries which are driven by short-term profitability. They may try to get away with as little expenditure as possible on environmental protection and have no serious commitment to the development of harmonious community relations. But with rare exceptions (at least in recent decades), these tend to be relatively small companies rather than those built over several generations. The latter should be, and generally are, much more concerned about long-term value creation. Corporate reputation vis-à-vis host governments and local communities, environmental performance and ethical behaviour play a key part in achieving success and, at a less philosophical level, are a means of managing risk.

At this particular time, in the midst of the worst recession we have seen in more than seventy years, there is widespread public distrust of the corporate world. The recession has been induced, at least in part, by reckless behaviour by a small section of the banking community. The amount of public funding which has been required to support the banks has been on an unthinkable scale. The public mood, whipped up by elements in the media, is hostile not just to those directly involved but to the whole banking sector and, by extension, to the rest of the business community. The personal avarice and risky, short-sighted behaviour of a few are thought by some to characterise all business leaders. Against this background, it is now more necessary than ever to make the case for Responsible Capitalism and to reinforce the values which the leaders of many of our major corporations maintain with great conviction.

At the same time as business has fallen into disrepute so, too, have politicians in the UK. This coincidence has resulted in politicians and business leaders alike being regarded with the level of cynicism once reserved for estate agents. I doubt that attitudes about either politicians or business leaders will be reversed by indignant exclamation that the problems are only caused by a small minority. Instead we should confront the criticisms more openly and work to identify and correct some of the root causes.

In the case of business we should acknowledge that many companies, sometimes unwittingly, have contributed to the attitudes and behaviours we all now decry. When companies establish remuneration systems which offer potentially huge short-term bonuses, they are implicitly encouraging precisely the reckless behaviour that has resulted. I hope that business leaders and the Boards of our large companies will reflect on and learn from the disastrous experiences of the past two years.

Regulatory issues aside, a single common factor which applies to all the financial services companies that have been bailed out appears to be their extraordinary reliance on massively disproportionate annual bonus schemes. Whilst not pretending that this has been the sole source of the financial hiatus, there is surely a causal relationship. It is, therefore, very disconcerting to hear that these reward systems seem to be re-emerging already in parts of the industry. I am not convinced that the policy of attaching claw-back conditions will do much to moderate the likelihood of risky behaviours. If I am right, then too much will depend, once again, on the effectiveness of the regulatory system.

Of course, businesses which adopt longer time horizons are also able to destroy value on a large scale but these are normally the consequence of errors of business judgement rather than defective reward structures. And even though we are seeing several governments intervene to prop up domestic motor industries, for example, the level of intervention is trivial in comparison with the banking sector. It is really only in the financial services area that corporate failures can be so great as to threaten the whole economic system. As the Governor of the Bank of England recently pointed out, the very notion that a company can be 'too big to fail' is a concept which is difficult to reconcile with the principles of a free market economy.

The example of what has gone wrong in the banking sector might well be taken as painful evidence that there is always need for a balance between profit and responsibility. Society as a whole now has to pay the price for what can happen when pursuit of profit overwhelms awareness of corporate responsibility.

I would argue, though, that the right question in the wake of our current economic woes is not so much the balance between profit and responsibility, but the correct balance between short and long-term profitability. Those who worship at the altar of quarterly results announcements and next week's share price are those who are susceptible to the behaviours that have wrought such great damage.

Add to these conditions a remuneration system largely reliant on short-term bonus payments and apply all this in companies that are 'too big to fail'. This constitutes a potent brew.

It may seem that I am arguing that industries like the extractives, with their long-lead time investments, are necessarily focused on long-term shareholder value and therefore have a greater incentive to behave in a responsible way than those in industries with shorter time horizons. This, though, is not the whole story.

If we look at some of the most familiar high street names, say Marks & Spencer or Waitrose, it is very obvious that great value attaches to the reputations that they have built up over generations. It would be little short of madness if the management of those companies were to choose to sacrifice reputation and customer goodwill by trying to raise near term profitability by acting in a way which would be deemed irresponsible. The same applies to consumer goods producers where great value is attached to brands. In this sense, at least, corporate responsibility can be seen as enlightened self-interest.

It is difficult to debate matters concerning 'corporate responsibility' without recognising that the term itself is subject to many definitions and that views about corporate responsibility and the standards they imply have changed considerably over time. Society's values change over time in almost every respect and it is no more appropriate to judge the corporate behaviour of the early twentieth century by today's standards, than it would be to judge any other aspect of social behaviour in one period by the values of another. In today's world though, corporate responsibility does not simply equate to philanthropy.

I need to extend this discussion of philanthropy a little because there is sometimes a close similarity between corporate support for local communities in education, health, the arts or provision of civic faculties and what I would regard as pure philanthropy (which is wholly unrelated to either a company's activities or the places where it operates). In the current economic environment, social needs are escalating and I would certainly not want to imply disapproval of companies acting as good corporate citizens. It is precisely in these times of hardship when corporate social budgets will be under pressure at the same time as the need for them is rising.

In drawing this to a conclusion, I would say that, today, the vision in many of our best large companies has more to do with 'sustainable development' than simple philanthropy. 'Sustainable development' is, of course, another of those terms capable of many definitions but all of them, I think, encompass the same principal challenges – environmental protection; economic development; and social development. Responsible corporate decision-making should take account of each of these aspects of sustainable development but, above all, companies should adhere faithfully to a value system which prizes integrity, at all times rejects corruption in any form, and which consistently demonstrates ethical awareness.

RESPONSIBLE CAPITALISM

THE RT HON Gordon Brown MP, THE RT HON Sir Don McKinnon GCVO, Rupert Goodman and Lord Dahrendorf KBE FBA in 2000

From left to right, back then front: Lord Plant of Highfield; Sir Patrick Cormack FSA MP; THE MOST REV AND THE RT HON Archbishop of Canterbury; Rupert Goodman; HON Raymond Seitz, Chief Emeka Anyaoku GCVO TC CFR; Dr Daniel Vasella, Chairman and CEO of Novartis; Lord Browne of Madingley; and Lord Dahrendorf KBE FBA (2000)

Above: From left to right, from back: Lord Marshall of Knightsbridge, Rupert Goodman, Sir Robert Wilson KCMG, THE RT HON Lord Howe of Aberavon CH QC and Jaime Zobel de Ayala, Chairman, Ayala Corporation (winner 2004)

Left: Lord Dahrendorf KBE speaks at the FIRST Responsible Capitalism Award ceremony in 2008

RESPONSIBLE CAPITALISM

Above: Rupert Goodman, Chairman, FIRST and Mr Ratan Tata, Chairman, Tata Sons

Left: HRH The Princess Royal at the FIRST Award ceremony in 2006

Above: Thomas Bata, Chairman, Bata Shoe Foundation, Sir Patrick Cormack FSA MP, THE RT HON Alistair Darling MP, Chancellor of the Exchequer, THE RT HON Lord Woolf of Barnes and Howard Schultz, Chairman, Starbucks Coffee Company

Above right: Rupert Goodman and HE Kamalesh Sharma, Commonwealth Secretary General

Below right: Sir Sigmund Sternberg, co-founder of the Three Faiths Forum receives the 2008 award from THE RT HON David Miliband MP Secretary of State for Foreign and Commonwealth Affairs

RESPONSIBLE CAPITALISM

Above: Rupert Goodman and THE RT HON David Miliband MP, Secretary of State for Foreign and Commonwealth Affairs

Above right: THE RT HON Lord Howe of Aberavon CH QC

Right: Sir Patrick Cormack FSA MP

THE RT HON Lord Woolf of Barnes, Chairman, FIRST Judging Panel

THE RT HON Lord Howe of Aberavon CH QC, Ms Hadeel Ibrahim, THE RT HON David Miliband MP and Lord Dahrendorf KBE in 2008

RESPONSIBLE CAPITALISM

1 THE RT HON Lord Woolf of Barnes, Lord Chief Justice of England and Wales, presenter in 2004

2 Morris Tabaksblat KBE, Chairman, Reed Elsevier, winner 2004

3 MOST REV AND THE RT HON Dr Rowan Williams, Archbishop of Canterbury, presenter 2003

4 Dr Daniel Vasella, Chairman and CEO, Novartis AG, winner 2003

5 THE RT HON Patricia Hewitt MP, Secretary of State for Trade and Industry, presenter 2002

6 Sir Robert Wilson KCMG, when Executive Chairman of Rio Tinto, winner 2002

7 THE RT HON Jack Straw MP, Secretary of State for Foreign and Commonwealth Affairs, presenter 2001

8 Marilyn Carlson Nelson, Chair and CEO, Carlson Companies, winner 2001

9 THE RT HON Alistair Darling MP, Chancellor of the Exchequer and Howard Schultz, Chairman, Starbucks Coffee Company, winner 2007

10 General Sir Mike Jackson GCB CBE DSO ADC GEN, Chief of the General Staff and Alan Wood CBE, Chief Executive, Siemens plc, winner 2005

11 HRH The Princess Royal, Sir Patrick Cormack FSA MP and Ratan Tata, Chairman, Tata Sons, winner 2006

CHAPTER EIGHT

RESPONSIBLE CAPITALISM IN CONFLICT AND POST-CONFLICT REGIONS

DR MOHAMED IBRAHIM

ONE OF THE CLEAREST ILLUSTRATIONS for me of the difference between responsible capitalism and its inverse, irresponsible capitalism, comes from my experience of doing business in conflict and post-conflict countries. Much has been written elsewhere of the negative impact of resource extraction during conflict and of the complicity of many multinational corporations in the perpetuation of conflict in order to secure resources. But when the mobile phone operator that I founded, Celtel International, acquired licences to operate in three countries that were emerging from conflict, we were able to contribute positively to the economies of these countries and ultimately to the perpetuation of peace. In Congo-Brazzaville, poor security status and lack of communication infrastructure meant that the United Nations (UN) was unwilling to allow its personnel to enter the country. Once we invested there in 1999, the security status of the country was immediately upgraded. In Kono, Sierra Leone, before our arrival there had been one expensive and unreliable satellite phone. Once Celtel made mobile phones more readily available, people's lives – from the fish vendor who could now do business better to the man who could get in touch with his relatives – were transformed. As security returned and we were able to expand our coverage in the country, we began to pay substantial sums of money to the government in income tax and licence fees helping to support this newly peaceful nation to rebuild its institutions. So even though we were operating in difficult conditions, in countries with huge security risks, we did not contribute in any way to exacerbating those conflicts but instead were able to do successful, clean business that supported these countries to continue on the path to peace. We grew our business while making an important contribution to the community.

I founded Celtel International in 1998. My experience had led me to believe that there was great potential in creating a pan-African mobile phone operator. So I pulled together a board of heavyweights from the telecoms and business worlds and began the process of acquiring operator licences on the continent.

Straight from the outset our board identified four key constituencies or stakeholders for our business: the shareholders, the employees, the customers, and the communities in which we operated. Each stakeholder would have to be considered when developing business plans and implementing our activities. As we moved forward with Celtel we continued to grow, with operations in 15 countries. And in all of them we continued to place this emphasis, we asked every single chief executive to report to us on how they were implementing this policy.

For the shareholders we operated as any business should. We were confident that we were in a high growth market with massive potential and we had a vision to become a major pan-African company. So we aggressively pursued licences, even in difficult operating environments such as Sierra Leone, Congo-Brazzaville and the Democratic Republic of the Congo. However, we were also cautious and kept our hands clean and costs down by refusing to pay bribes. And we were constantly adapting the kinds of products we were providing to better suit our context. Although many of these innovations benefited our customers, they also had the added advantage of exponentially increasing our revenue. For example, the move to provide mobile phone airtime via small denominations through prepaid scratch cards has revolutionised the customer base for mobile phones in Africa. In the end, our shareholders' return averaged eight times their investment, respectable returns by any standard.

Our objective was always to build, operate and market a pan-African mobile network. We needed the scale which would allow us to reduce our operating costs and, crucially, our procurement costs. This issue of scale is one key problem which will always impact the commercial viability of such enterprises in many African countries. We adopted a "one network" approach as far as we could, navigating our way through the very diverse and sometimes complicated regulatory regimes in our countries. Frankly, I was surprised by the many political and regulatory hurdles we faced. Unfortunately African governments are yet to embrace seriously regional economic integration as an essential prerequisite to the development of their economies. On the commercial side we developed the Celtel brand across our operations. We chose to emphasise a new image of Africa as a continent on the move, using images of young African professionals. Our branding substantially increased our profits but also helped to improve perceptions of Africa. Years of predominantly negative imagery of the continent had taken its toll both within and externally, with many perceiving Africa as a basket case continent. Young Africans needed to see a different image of themselves and their potential, as did their international partners.

We also pioneered the concept of cost-free roaming between our operations in Africa. Pre-paid and post paid. Again in the face of some unhelpful regulatory hurdles!

The vast majority (over 98%) of our employees were Africans. Since we were introducing a new complex technology and a new business model, in the newly liberalised telecoms sector, we needed to embark on major training programmes for our employees. For training our engineers and technicians we relied mainly on our suppliers (Ericsson, Siemens, etc) while London Business School designed and ran special training programmes for our senior and middle managers.

We instilled a sense of shared values and common purpose throughout the company and backed this up by offering employees the chance to own shares in the business. In all of my businesses I have always insisted on this as an important way of creating commitment and a reward mechanism for the people who have journeyed with you, who have taken risks, worked their hardest, and built the success story. When we sold Celtel in 2005, 15% of the company shares were held by its employees.

Rolling out and operating our vast infrastructure, created huge business opportunities for local entrepreneurs. We procured steel towers, furniture, cables, office equipment and supplies etc locally. We outsourced all civil works and most maintenance functions. We had many thousands of towers for our base stations, with a huge number of electric generators and batteries requiring daily attention. All sales activities were outsourced to retailers and vendors. Excluding Nigeria, for which I have no figures, we had well over 140 000 points of sale (essentially a kiosk on the roadside selling our scratch-cards). In Kinshasa alone there were some 20,000 such points of sale. We really helped support a huge number of young entrepreneurs in our countries.

We always had a zero-tolerance policy towards corruption and bribery and ensured that our managers had support in implementing this. No manager was authorised to make a payment above $30,000 without board approval. This protected managers if they came under pressure. It is important to make the point here that business is as much responsible as the few government officials for the cancer of bribery in Africa. Both must take a stand against it.

However all of these were part of the indirect programme of engaging and benefitting local communities. We also pioneered Corporate Social Responsibility (CSR) schemes in Africa that were specifically directed at local communities. Our two main areas of focus have been education, to train aspiring leaders for the African continent, and fostering social cohesion in Africa's diverse and sometimes polarised countries. We have set up scholarship schemes and donated educational resources in support of the Millennium Development Goals, as well as creating cultural events and programmes that underline the importance of unity and harmony in our societies.

Looking back I feel proud of what we accomplished with Celtel, we can really say that we changed people's lives for the better. And when we sold the business in 2005 that was not the end of the story for me. I have taken the money I made and started my Foundation which promotes and facilitates improved governance in Africa. The Foundation is focused on two core initiatives, an annual index of African governance that is designed to provide a tool for civil society and citizens to hold governments to account, and the largest annually awarded prize in the world, which recognises achievement and excellence in African leadership. So I am using my business success to re-invest back into my continent and tackle an issue that I feel is the single most important challenge facing the African continent.

CHAPTER NINE

RESPONSIBLE CAPITALISM – THE CONTINENTAL EUROPEAN MODEL

DR DANIEL VASELLA

IT MAY CURRENTLY APPEAR, in the course of the financial market crisis and the moves to overcome it through economic stimulus packages, as if the US is acting in a more statist manner than Europe, which traditionally leans towards a stronger state.

However, this situation is unlikely to continue for any length of time owing to the huge differences in political culture on the two sides of the Atlantic. The Anglo-American economic model places more trust in the markets and individuals and tolerates a greater degree of social inequality. The continental European economic model, on the other hand, is characterised by a degree of scepticism towards the market, and makes greater efforts to achieve as equal access as possible to healthcare and education. Of course, theory and reality sometimes differ considerably on both sides of the Atlantic.

Needless to say, shareholder value thinking has never been as strong in continental Europe as in the Anglo-Saxon world. The more sustainable stakeholder capitalism is deeper rooted here, although this is naturally a simplified comparison and is even somewhat flattering to Europe. As is well known, Europe still has much to learn from America as regards the importance and appreciation of innovation and entrepreneurial initiative.

If European stakeholder capitalism is, however, truly focused on real long-term value creation and is not simply the path of least resistance against stakeholder groups, this model and its long-term focus should be welcomed; spontaneous (and fast-fading) applause from the stock exchange should not be the only criterion for the economy, as it leads to decisions being taken that are not in the interests of long-term corporate success for the sake of maximising share prices in the short term.

These differences between the continental European and Anglo-Saxon economic models that have emerged over centuries will probably never fully disappear.

Nonetheless, there is a certain degree of convergence: One of the prime objectives of the Obama administration is to expand health coverage to the more than 40 million Americans who to date have been at risk of sliding all too easily into hardship when they fall ill. In Europe, belief in the welfare state, which helped to support national identities on an insecure continent from the end of the Second World War, has been crumbling for some time now. The view of the comprehensive welfare state now is that it is too costly and often counterproductive; the trend is, rationally, towards an active welfare state that offers incentives, making work worthwhile. Both trends are part of a larger movement towards more responsible and sustainable capitalism.

This gradual convergence is a result of the common challenges of globalisation, which poses the question for all political models of how a country can be made as attractive as possible without endangering social cohesion.

The pragmatic response to these challenges, both here and on the other side of the Atlantic, gives cause for confidence as we will not be able to tackle large, global problems in a way that promises success without changing the way we think. More than that, we will all have to do away with ingrained ways of thinking and political myths. There is no alternative: the world is getting smaller, for better or for worse. Anyone who ignores this fact does so at their own – political and ethical – risk.

As for the political systems in Western countries, the motto here too must be that we only have a chance if we approach these challenges pragmatically. If we insist on drawing a line between ourselves and others, we will fail. The only truly interesting questions in development and healthcare policy are: What are our ultimate objectives? Who is taking on what role? What do governments need to do? What about international organisations such as the World Health Organisation (WHO)? What contribution can non-governmental organisations (NGOs) make? And what responsibility do companies have?

If the term 'responsible capitalism' is truly to mean something, then all players must assume their individual responsibilities. This is also clear from healthcare provision in extremely poor countries without a functioning healthcare system.

The main difficulty here is a political one: Unprofessional governance, and often even governmental indifference to the suffering of its own people, is not uncommon in the countries concerned. The economy here is reliant on committed and persistent support from Western governments. Even NGOs, with their huge commitment to, and their frequently outstanding knowledge of, individual regions and problem areas, play a central role. Whether it's a matter of good governance and tackling corruption, or infrastructure, i.e. clean drinking water and hospitals, the economy cannot lay the foundations for their action alone.

My hope is for progress that will introduce to the debate strong business acumen and a well-developed awareness of human suffering as well as a sense of what can really be achieved. As the economist Jeffrey Sachs said recently: "Companies are only successful if they have a business plan and are committed to economic viability. Their primary focus is on results and how to achieve them. It should be exactly the same in the case of development aid."

This seems to me to be more correct and true today than ever before. The epicentre of the current global economic crisis is in affluent countries. Every one of us must do whatever we can to ensure that it is not the poorest who are the hardest hit by its consequences. It will now become apparent which companies take social responsibility seriously, and which do not, as well as which countries are really prepared to help developing countries, and which are not. At its heart, the financial crisis is an ethical one. We will only emerge from it by acting ethically. What lies ahead is nothing less than a global litmus test for the 'responsible capitalism' that is so gladly and frequently evoked in after-dinner speeches.

The consequences of health problems in many developing countries are still barely conceivable for us. For example, every 30 seconds, a child dies of malaria in Africa.

As a responsible multinational company, Novartis feels an obligation to help as much as it can – regardless of the current operating cycle. Since 2001, as part of our malaria and leprosy programmes, we have already provided 250 million treatments without profit, thereby helping to save the lives of around 550,000 people. Our social commitment is a steadfast value – and an integral part of our strategy.

It is artificial to separate core business from social responsibility. As a pharma company, we bring products onto the market that can improve, prolong, and sometimes even save peoples' lives. Charles Handy neatly summarised the meaning of capitalism: "The purpose of a business is to make a profit so that the business can do something more or better." However, this definition of an economic school of thought that only focuses on figures down to the last decimal point underestimates capitalism (although it truly believes in its qualities).

Nonetheless, we must also play a part by putting forward our concerns, as this mechanism does not work in extremely poor markets. Pure PR measures will, however, become increasingly counterproductive for companies in the future. They will only make the European public, which is already more cynical about the economy than that in the US, increasingly cynical. And cynicism is the exact opposite of the mentality on which responsible capitalism is based: rational optimism.

We are facing a paradox: states are acting more prominently as regulators, but at the same time, they are more dependent than before on the contribution from the economy, as it is well known that public finances will remain stretched for some considerable time. However, this lamentable situation also presents an opportunity for the economy to prove itself a real partner for society and thus gradually win back the legitimacy it lost due to recklessness in certain financial circles.

CHAPTER TEN

RESPONSIBLE CAPITALISM AND THE COMMONWEALTH

HIS EXCELLENCY KAMALESH SHARMA

OVER THE TWO CENTURIES since the word was coined, capitalism has had a mixed press. Its critics have been particularly trenchant. As a result, whether it is the rapacious mill owners of 19th Century Lancashire so vitriolically lampooned by Karl Marx, or the self-lampooning of the larger-than-life figures of recent Wall Street scandals, responsibility and capitalism have not always seemed easy bedfellows.

However, it is important to recognise that abuse and excess are not the essence of capitalism. Capitalism is fundamentally anchored in the ability of individuals to realise their potential through an exercise of their individual rights. And the success of this approach has been seen, as capitalism has supported more prosperity for more people than any other system ever. Enterprise is the source of goods, services and jobs – and not only for the rich. Capitalism – and the dynamic private sector which it supports – has been responsible for lifting millions out of poverty across the world, to which the two emerging economic powerhouses of India and China bear the most eloquent of current testimonies. It is only through continuing to realise the potential of this system that our shared goal of eliminating absolute poverty can be achieved.

Within the Commonwealth – a diverse, voluntary association of 53 nations in all continents and embracing all cultures – there is recognition that whilst it is easy to equate capitalism with sharp suits and skyscrapers, the reality of capitalism for the majority of Commonwealth citizens lies in the small firms where families and neighbours work side-by-side. SMEs constitute almost 90% of most economies: they are the dynamos of growth. And now, nearly every nation on earth embraces some form of capitalism.

With examples of irresponsible capitalism so evident, the challenge is to recognise how ingredients which provide the strength of the capitalist system can be combined so that it works sustainably for all people. In other words, we are asking how to bring about a responsible – democratic – capitalism. The ingredients of economic development only take on real shape when they are made democratic. Hence the need to promote all business activity – as much for small businesses and women and youth entrepreneurs, as for big business. And hence, too, this need for responsible business – accountable socially and environmentally as well as financially. 'Good' business, they say, is good *for* business, and it is democracy that ought to lie at the root of capitalism.

The form of capitalism a society expresses reflects choices: by individuals and companies, through the exercise of their economic rights; by governments, as embodiments of the society's collective will; and, increasingly, by the international community as a group. It is the interaction of these three groups which defines the extent to which capitalism in all its forms is responsible or not.

It is government that sets the parameters within which any economic system works. The building blocks of efficient and responsible capitalism are amongst the fundamental responsibilities of any state. The first prerequisite is a system of respect for individual property rights through which the freedoms of individuals to trade goods, labour and services are protected. The second is a judicial system able to enforce these rights, on behalf of all.

The Commonwealth invests heavily in both these areas. Democracy at all levels of society – national, regional and local – ensures that the rights of all individuals are respected. Through the transparency and accountability of the democratic process, government becomes responsive to the needs of its citizens. The Commonwealth firmly sees a connection between this accountability, the safeguarding of individual rights, and economic and social development. Capitalism can only work where there is confidence in the future, and in the knowledge that investment today will be rewarded by the ability to realise a return on that investment tomorrow. Democratic accountability and an equitable judiciary together combine to provide a bulwark against the arbitrariness which can undermine that confidence. It also ensures that it is more profitable to build a business than to manipulate the political system based on patronage or corruption.

In the modern state, these two fundamental roles of government find a more elaborate expression in the form of regulation. On the one hand, regulation plays a permissive role. All governments have processes which need to be undertaken to set up and close down businesses. A key part of the vibrancy and effectiveness of the private sector is determined by these processes, and the state's role is to ensure that they are applied efficiently – balancing the need for protection of the public with releasing economic potential. Commonwealth countries have a good track record of delivery in this area: two members – Singapore and New Zealand – top the World Bank's 'Doing Business' rankings, and only two members lie in the bottom quartile. And increasingly, Commonwealth member governments commit to practising what they preach, for instance with Nigeria and Ghana committing to making public all their revenues for oil, gas and mining, under the UK-led Extractive Industries Transparency Initiative.

The Commonwealth plays a modest role in this achievement by providing support to implement best practice in supporting the business environment and strengthening the ability of small- and medium-sized firms to find the finance they need to grow, and to provide employment. It also plays a growing role in supporting governments in bringing young people within the economic system. More than half the Commonwealth's population is under 25. Commonwealth programmes support education in financial literacy, since an understanding of money, its potential and limitations, is a key step in the creation of economically responsible citizens. More fundamentally, the young are an untapped entrepreneurial resource, and the Commonwealth is looking to ways to engage and develop that potential. The Commonwealth Youth Credit Initiative has set up some 2,000 youth businesses: over 90% of loans made have been repaid, in a package that includes loans, skills-building, marketing and management, and business counselling and mentoring.

In addition to its permissive role, government has a vital function in establishing the hard boundaries to capitalism. This has been illustrated vividly in recent months with the debate over the role of government in the regulation of the financial sector. However, it applies at least equally to other forms of regulation, for example in health and safety and environmental protection. These regulatory norms are themselves expressions of a society's assessment of what activities and risks are acceptable. In all these ways – regulatory, legal and political – responsible capitalism is fundamentally supported by an efficient, transparent and accountable state.

Yet while governments may set the parameters within which capitalism operates, it is the millions of individual capitalists who bear the greatest burden for ensuring that capitalism operates responsibly. It is increasingly clear that responsible capitalism is about more than making money. Environmental sustainability underpins all human activity, but is literally undervalued in the current economic system. A responsible capitalism must continue to recognise that sustainable development must be secured, and that innovation will be needed to achieve it. As a result, in the same way as governments are accountable through openness and transparency, business needs also to be accountable for its environmental and social performance. Examples of ways in which this can be achieved can be seen across the full capitalist spectrum. In the largest companies of the world there is an increasing move towards recognising the value of the 'triple bottom line', through which environmental and social measures supplement the financial. At the other end of the scale, the philosophy underpinning the microcredit movement – where finance is put to the service of social objectives – demonstrates how innovative thinking can put responsibility where it should always be, at the heart of capitalism. And the Commonwealth family is supporting this effort as well. The attention paid by firms to their corporate social responsibility is an important manifestation of this greater attention to the obligations of businesses to the societies in which they operate.

For the Commonwealth, responsible capitalism is 'on the statute books'. The Commonwealth Business Council presented guidelines to Commonwealth Heads of Government in Abuja in 2003, and they were formally endorsed there. Those guidelines took the form of a so-called Joint Plan: six promises from Government, seven from Business, and two from Government and Business together. The Plan has been tested in Ghana, Mozambique and Tanzania – in each, a climate of dialogue has led to a climate of investment. Meanwhile, alongside the Joint Plan are the Commonwealth Business Council Guidelines for Corporate Citizenship – on company values, company corporate governance, company relationships, and the assessment of the different types of company impact.

The CBC itself gives practical support, and collects examples of best practice. It has amassed exceptional testimony from companies supporting health in the workplace and the community (from AIDS, to dental care, to water sanitation), and from companies supporting education and skills development, and the development of small enterprises. It has produced innovative analytical tools for helping its members understand and monitor their efforts in promoting corporate social responsibility.

So responsible capitalism must be inculcated by governments and companies. So, too, must it be established as a shared goal for the international community.

As the world becomes increasingly economically and culturally interconnected, ensuring responsible capitalism becomes an international as well as a national obligation. Commonwealth countries are more fully integrated with the global trading and financial system than others. As a result, the membership is genuinely committed to finding multilateral solutions to global challenges. Neither individual Commonwealth members, nor the Commonwealth as a group, can solve these problems alone. As a result, the Commonwealth recognises that responsible capitalism is best supported by a rules-based international system. This is particularly true of the global trading system. Rules provide protection for small countries – which form 32 of the Commonwealth's members. Without the ability to exchange goods and services through trade, there can be no capitalism. A responsible global capitalism requires a successful conclusion to the Doha Round of trade negotiations, which genuinely benefits developing countries and which recognises the particular challenges faced by small states. Only an equitable outcome will be for the benefit of all.

But the need for effective multilateralism to support responsible capitalism is wider and deeper than this. For illustration, we look no further than the mismatch between global financial flows and national financial regulation in the current economic and financial crisis. Here, and more generally, there is a need for effective international institutions to support multilateral cooperation. Commonwealth leaders are fully committed to strengthening the effectiveness of the global institutions, and in June 2008 set out principles to guide the reform and promote these institutions' transparency, effectiveness and – above all – their inclusiveness. Their hope is to move the world from a narrow globalisation to a shared globalism, in which all can realise the benefits of responsible capitalism.

It may seem that in the past two years there has been a serious challenge to capitalism as the dominant model of economic development. That would be to underestimate its underlying strength. However, what has been learned is not that capitalism has failed, but rather that it needs nurturing and guiding to prevent its successes becoming excesses. For millions of people striving to reach their potential and to achieve greater prosperity, it remains responsible capitalism that has the greatest ability to fulfil those hopes.

CHAPTER ELEVEN

CAN RESPONSIBLE CAPITALISM HELP AFRICA'S PROSPERITY?

CHIEF EMEKA ANYAOKU GCVO TC CFR

IN 1989 THE FALL OF THE BERLIN WALL not only marked a major milestone in the advance of political freedom but also de-legitimised communism – in particular its central planning process – as a mechanism for economic organisation. In 2009, the deepening global economic and financial crisis has raised questions about whether capitalism is about to witness a similar fate. It is capitalism's nature to reveal its weaknesses from time to time, triggering corrective measures. Indeed, the resilience of capitalism as a mechanism for organising the economy has arisen from its adaptive nature, which is why there are many varieties of capitalism, albeit with certain common characteristics. To appreciate whether responsible capitalism can help generate prosperity in Africa, it helps both to explain the foundations and forms of capitalism and to examine Africa's progress towards creating those foundations.

Foundations and Forms of Capitalism

Capitalism rests on two foundations: the institutional and the technical. The institutional foundations of capitalism include respect for private property;

rule of law, often expressed in an effective legal and regulatory framework; and a sound financial system. The institutional foundations of capitalism, and hence for prosperity, were articulated by Adam Smith, when he wrote in his *Wealth of Nations* that "little is required to carry a state to the highest opulence but peace, easy taxes and a tolerable administration of justice". Thus, in that short sentence, the need for political stability, sound public finance and rule of law was underlined as pre-requisites for prosperity.

Equally important are the technical foundations of capitalism. These include high literacy rate, critical mass of technical expertise (in particular in sciences, engineering, medicine and management) and entrepreneurial risk-taking and innovation. In country after country where capitalism has thrived, the winning formula has consisted of developing both the institutional and technical foundations. No country can make much progress in generating prosperity by focusing only on developing and strengthening the institutional or the technical foundations of capitalism. Both must go together.

The variations in forms of capitalism stem both from how the fruits of prosperity are distributed in society and how the firm – the basic unit of production – is organised. Mainly, there are three varieties of capitalism: market capitalism, state capitalism and social market capitalism. In market capitalism, the market mechanism is the means of allocating resources to factors of production, for distributing the rewards of prosperity and the firm is privately owned mainly through shareholding. By contrast, in social market capitalism – often also referred to as social democracy – while the market mechanism is the means of allocating resources to the factors of production and the firm is privately owned, the distribution of rewards of prosperity is a product of public policy and not market-based. On the other hand, in state capitalism, while the firms may be state-owned, the allocation of resources is through the market mechanism.

Africa's progress in laying the foundations of capitalism

African countries have had a mixed record in laying the foundations for capitalism. This is at once a recognition of the diversity of historical experiences among the African countries, as it is of the diversity in their current conditions. The diversity of experience stemmed from the role and reach of the state in individual African countries. At independence, most African countries were orientated politically towards democracy and economically towards the market.

Over time, marked differences began to emerge; so much so that by 1982, in his book *Ideology and Development in Africa*, the American political scientist Crawford Young would classify African countries into three categories by the then prevailing regime types: "Afro-Marxists, Popular Socialists and African Capitalists". Of course, these regime types had important implications for the organisation of the economy in each country. Not surprisingly, in the Afro-Marxists and Popular Socialists states, there were no stock markets, rule of law was weak and private property was not looked upon favourably. By contrast, in the African capitalist countries, both domestic and foreign investment were encouraged, stock markets existed and there was a legal and regulatory framework that supported private property rights.

However, the ideological facades concealed many common characteristics across the spectrum of countries. Typically, all had weak institutional foundations for capitalism, all had even much weaker technical foundations and many suffered political instability. More importantly, all relied fairly extensively on state-owned enterprises as the main unit of production, especially in the so-called "commanding heights" of the economy. The economic reforms that African countries embarked upon from the mid-1980s were aimed in part to redefine the role and reach of the state, in particular by privatising state-owned enterprises; in part to promote sound macro-economic policy; and in part to make the economies more market friendly – in other words to pave the way for market capitalism.

If the economic reforms efforts have not achieved much progress in creating the foundations for capitalism after nearly 25 years, it is not because of lack of awareness and efforts in supporting institutional foundations of capitalism in Africa. Instead, it is because not much progress has been made in creating the technical foundations of capitalism: increasing literacy rate; producing a critical mass of technical expertise in the sciences, engineering, medicine and management; and developing a culture of entrepreneurial risk-taking and innovation.

Although African entrepreneurial flair is in abundant display in the vibrant informal sector throughout the region, no modern economy can rely on the informal sector as the main driver of economic growth and development. The typical informal sector enterprise represents a melding of "economy of affection" practices with vigorous individual efforts. In that sense, capitalism in the African context is not the absence of entrepreneurial and risk-taking orientation but the inability to take many sole proprietor or family-owned enterprises from take-off through consolidation to maturity. Yet, mortality rates among informal sector and family-owned businesses are high. The main challenge, therefore, is how to transform the informal sector enterprises into formal enterprises that are managed on modern management principles and practices.

Many factors are implicated in the lack of significant progress in creating the institutional and technical foundations of capitalism. Notably, these include political instability and conflicts, corruption, inadequate investments in producing critical mass of technical expertise and low investment in infrastructure. Development assistance – which has been alternately praised by its supporters and condemned by critics – has not been particularly helpful in creating the foundations of capitalism. This is not to say that aid has not been useful or cannot be potentially helpful. Instead, the problem has been in the composition of aid in Africa.

Several studies have shown that significant shares of aid resources are not directed to those areas that could strengthen the institutional and technical foundations of capitalism in Africa. For example, well over 40 percent of aid to Africa is devoted to technical cooperation, developmental food aid, emergency aid, grants for debt forgiveness, and assistance channelled through non-governmental organisations. The need to channel aid to areas that can create Africa's capacity to grow ought to provide a unifying theme for advocates and critics of aid in Africa.

Yet it would be wrong to conclude that Africa is not taking incipient steps towards creating modern capitalist enterprises. The stirrings of such efforts can be found in the growing telecommunications sector, in the rapidly expanding financial services sector and in the nimble tourism sector across Africa. The experience gained from managing the firms in these sectors will undoubtedly provide invaluable insights into creating wealth in the region. After decades of state-dominated economies, private sector led growth is all the rage in the region and that imposes a different set of obligations on the state, as will be explained shortly.

Creating Wealth Responsibly

Creating wealth is capitalism's great boast and its comparative advantage over defunct ideologies. Generating prosperity, however, requires economic growth, which depends on increased productivity, which in turn requires a range of technical skills, and which comes from quality human capital formation. As the basic unit of production in capitalism, the privately-owned firm is responsible for producing goods and services. To survive, the private firm must produce efficiently and earn profits. Sustained profits are the oxygen of capitalism. Hence, capitalism's harsh and brutal face is linked to the perpetual search for higher and higher profits.

The pursuit of profit can trample on moral and social imperatives of society. This raises the question whether capitalism can be responsible and whether it can help Africa. The answers to both questions are in the affirmative. Successful capitalism occurs only in the context of profitability of firms, for an unprofitable firm dies in no time. Responsible capitalism refers to corporate conduct that includes complying with the laws of the country, refraining from any acts that harm the environment, impair the health of the people or denigrate their culture; and making social investments in the host communities. The term of art for this type of conduct is good corporate citizenship, which at once reconciles the need for profit-making with ethical behaviour and corporate social responsibility. The concept of corporate social responsibility is broad. It encompasses not only charitable acts by the firm but also economically empowering people in the host communities by purchasing their goods and services and employing people from such communities.

Ensuring responsible capitalism is a task for both domestic and transnational firms operating in Africa and for the state. In as much as the foreign multinational firms in Africa have played a dominant role in Africa, the burden of proof for responsible capitalism falls disproportionately on them. In many important respects, however, the corporate conduct of some foreign firms in Africa has fallen far short of good corporate citizenship. They have polluted the environment, failed to make significant social investments in their host communities, exploited and sought to benefit from mineral resources in situations of conflict (remember the taint of "conflict-diamonds") and have been complicit in human rights violation and repression and in bribing political leaders and elites.

In the past decade, a number of guidelines have been developed to foster responsible capitalism. These have mainly taken the forms of voluntary codes of conduct which subscribing firms and other economic agents are required to adhere. The most prominent of these are the United Nations inspired Global Compact aimed at making firms adhere to a set of principles in human rights, labour standards, environment protection and anti-corruption; the Extractive Industries Transparency Initiative aimed at promoting greater transparency in the transactions in the mining and energy sectors; the Kimberley process designed to combat illegal trafficking of diamonds from conflict zones; and the Equator principles aimed at incorporating environmental and social considerations in the financial services sector.

African governments have a sovereign duty to provide an enabling environment for private firms to flourish. But that duty also includes ensuring that private firms strictly adhere to all relevant laws. The inability or unwillingness of some African governments to monitor and enforce compliance to a host of national laws by private firms, in particular the multinationals in their countries, have left their citizens to wonder whether capitalism can bring prosperity to them.

Responsible capitalism that engenders prosperity does not emerge spontaneously. It is rather fostered by a combination of a set of effective policies and practices: It is a product of competitive and profitable firms, operating in a stable political environment in the context of sound legal and regulatory framework complemented by political and moral exhortations expressed in a web of voluntary codes of conduct.

Today, as Ejeviome Eloho Otobo wrote in his article "Recognise efforts to strengthen democracy in Africa" in the *Financial Times* of 27th December 2006, "the 53 African countries can be classified into four categories according to where they lie on the peace and development spectrum: those still in conflict; those emerging from conflict; those where democratic stability is racked by disruptive political tensions and undermined by weak institutions and governance practices; and those where democratic consolidation is buttressed by stable economic growth". The prospects that responsible capitalism can generate prosperity in Africa are highest in the last category of countries.

CHAPTER TWELVE

CHINA: CAN CAPITALISM CONTINUE TO FLOURISH RESPONSIBLY?

THE RT HON THE LORD HOWE OF ABERAVON CH QC

To anyone with a sense of history, China's achievements over the past 30 years have been truly impressive. China's far-sighted leader, Deng Xiaoping, could not have foreseen how extraordinary the growth of China's economy has been since he first introduced economic reform in 1979. But he could see that the model of a wholly state-controlled economy was not serving China's needs and that elements of capitalism had to be introduced. His open-door policy, and his philosophy that it mattered not if the cat was black or white as long as it caught the mouse, have led to the development of an economy that many would recognise as capitalist in all but name. Yet the current financial crisis has also demonstrated the sharp differences that do still exist between China's market economy with Chinese characteristics and the highly developed market economies in the West.

Since the start of economic reforms from 1978 onwards the statistics are staggering. Somewhere in the order of 200-300 million people have been lifted out of poverty. Sustained economic growth has averaged over 9% a year over three decades and this year China is expected to overtake Japan as the world's second largest economy in terms of the size of its

RESPONSIBLE CAPITALISM

GDP. Of course, GDP per capita in China has a long way to go. As Prime Minister Wen Jiabao pointed out in his recent Cambridge speech, it still ranks behind 100 other countries – at only about one eighteenth that of Britain. But its economy has risen impressively and China's economic progress has undoubtedly improved the standard of living of most of its 1.3 billion people, even if the progress has not been even.

All through the reform period of the past 30 years there has been an underlying sense that China has been playing catch-up with the West and there has been no shortage of advice to the Chinese as to how to reform and develop their economy. Until very recently Western financiers were lecturing China on the need to further reform their banks and loosen state control. Some of that advice is looking less robust in the light of the global economic crisis that was caused by the irresponsible behaviour of banks in the US and the level of risk they took. Indeed many in China have enjoyed a certain sense of smugness, as their more cautious pace in financial reform appears to have shielded China from the worst affects of the financial crisis.

So, with predictions very recently from the World Bank that China's economy would perform better at 7.1% than previously assessed at around 6% and that it is likely to become the world's second largest economy, there are many reasons why China is feeling increasingly confident about its own path. And to many Chinese, conscious of the 5,000-year history of Chinese civilisation, China is simply on its way back to its rightful and proper place at or close to the top of the world economic order. As economic historians testify, China had the world's largest economy for much of recorded history, until the industrial revolution in Europe catapulted the Europeans and Americans ahead. Even as late as 1820, China accounted for a third of global GDP.

Has this path been that of what might be termed "responsible capitalism"? In certain respects China has certainly been responsible. In spite of the many pressures, largely from the international community, to accelerate the pace and nature of its economic reform China has actually taken a very measured approach to its economic, legal and political reforms. To quote Deng again, China is very much "crossing the river by feeling for the stones"- or Wen

Jiabao "a country constantly developing and changing". The gradual liberalisation and privatisation of parts of the Chinese economy in a series of phases, starting with the agricultural reforms of the '80s and the first development of a free market, a move away from a patriarchal system to one now described as a "socialist market economy", where there can be bankruptcies, workers can be hired and fired and shares in companies can be traded on the domestic and in some cases international stock markets – this gradual approach has avoided what many would call the chaos of the post-Soviet economies and certainly the pain of those sharp adjustments. China behaved very responsibly during the Asian financial crisis of the late '90s and is credited with helping to secure regional stability by not devaluing the Yuan. This year many are looking to China as the possible saviour economy during the economic downturn. And with its 4.1 trillion Yuan domestic stimulus programme, and the use of sovereign wealth funds to invest in Europe and elsewhere, China is certainly playing a part in stabilising the global economic picture. In 2007 – the last year for which information is available – the UK was the number one destination for Chinese investment in the EU; and UK remains the largest EU investor in China.

Last year's anniversary of 30 years of opening up and reform celebrated justifiably the overall success of this approach, whilst recognising that there are many problems. Inequalities and divergences have grown between urban and rural, between the east coast and the western hinterland and these create challenges to the Chinese government, in terms of the future, of how the benefits of economic development are enjoyed and by whom; and in terms of social harmony – a theme close to the present Chinese leadership's heart.

Whilst overall China is to be applauded for its responsible approach, and indeed many are looking at China to see if it provides a replicable development model for other countries, most notably in Africa, there has been nevertheless a high cost. The pollution in many of China's cities is causing serious respiratory problems to their residents and China overtook the US as the greatest emitter of greenhouse gases last year; nearly 70% of China's waters, both rivers and lakes, are intolerably unclean with over half of the largest cities facing water shortages; and an area about the size of Ulster is lost each year to desertification.

The working conditions for many Chinese labourers are far from meeting the ILO standards generally accepted as a minimum. The frequent reports of the injuries and even deaths of miners and factory workers are a constant reminder that in a country the size of China there are still enormous discrepancies in health and safety standards. China has yet to allow a free trade union movement, even if the role of the All China Federation of Trade Unions is moving closer to a better representation of workers' interests. And there are many other issues with standards, such as food and drug safety, and the rampant exploitation of IPR, that indicate that the Chinese economy still has many irresponsible aspects.

So if one accepts that China has moved from a highly patriarchal economy, where all the citizens' basic needs were met, to one where capitalist practices have been encouraged, including private ownership and a greater, but still not complete, role for the market, are the signs good or bad for China's continued economic growth being responsible? To quote Prime Minister Wen again: "The invisible hand of the market and the visible hand of government and social supervision should both act, and act vigorously".

The answer in practice is, of course, a qualified one. There have been some impressive legal reforms, including most recently the Labour Contract Law which, after highly contentious debates between not just Chinese interests but also international lobbyists and labour organisations, gives much more protection to workers' rights including against unfair dismissal and setting some minimum wage standards. The government has no plans to dilute the law even in the face of the pressures of a slowdown in the economy because, as it argues, although labour costs have risen as a result of the law, the number of labour disputes has declined and this is the overriding priority.

China is also showing a cautiously responsible attitude to the environment. The Chinese government acknowledges the severity of climate change, the risks to the economy and the well-being of its population. It does this in the context that it has the same right to develop as do industrialised countries and that one-third of its emissions originates from commodities produced in China but exported to other countries. And it is taking measures to reduce energy consumption, both for cost and supply reasons as well as for environmental protection reasons. It will be very interesting to see how the debate between developing and developed nations plays out at Copenhagen and in the post-2012 negotiations. The issue in terms of making a genuine impact on China's environmental damage will remain one of political will – and the ability of the government to enforce domestically the commitments it undertakes internationally. It will also depend, as Pan Yue, Deputy Head of China's Environmental Protection Agency, has pointed out, on the ability of civil society to hold the mainly state-owned polluting industries to account.

Another area where there are signs of a more responsible approach is the growth of the corporate social responsibility agenda within China itself. CSR is itself an extremely broad term and covers many aspects of good corporate behaviour, from treating staff fairly to giving money to the poor and helping local society. The Sichuan Earthquake last year indicated how far the Chinese corporate world had moved, as it responded generously with money and staff time to help the victims. To quote Prime Minister Wen: "We should call on all enterprises to take up their social responsibilities. Within the body of every businessman should flow the blood of morality". Sichuan was also a turning point in many respects in the attitude of the Chinese government to the involvement of civil society organisations in the delivery of basic services. And there is evidence of a growing engagement by local governments at the grassroots level looking to work more closely with Chinese non-governmental organisations on health and education issues.

There are probably still serious distortions in the Chinese economy that will need to be addressed in the medium term. For instance, China's much trumpeted reserves are not so much, (as one leading Chinese economist, Fan Gang, has shown), a result of the high rate of individual savings – these have, as his research shows, stayed relatively stable over the past twenty years – but a result of the large reserves held by state-owned corporations. The question of full privatisation of core industries such as oil and gas is very problematic and the time may not yet be right. But there are strong arguments for China at least addressing the issue and facing the necessity of letting the real price of energy enter the market.

So there are still major challenges facing China and its continued development. China still needs to create another 200 million new jobs to keep its workforce fully employed. Currently 20 million migrant workers have returned to their hometowns without finding new employment. China's banking sector, in spite of its relative strength during this financial crisis, still faces serious questions of reform and expertise. Although there are signs of a growing plurality in China, there are still, in fully mercantilist eyes, some serious shortcomings in the Chinese system that may inhibit long-term sustainable economic growth. If China is to continue to meet its people's expectation of economic growth it will need to do so responsibly and it may mean tackling some very sensitive issues. And in the end China may need to face the political reform questions that many would say are an inevitable next step. There is an interdependence between effective company auditing, reliable official statistics, independent trade unions and strong corporate governance and freedom of expression, security from arbitrary arrest and detention without trial, which is not always obvious to economists but would certainly fall within my understanding of responsible capitalism.

Three decades have now passed since Deng Xiaoping first set China on the path of economic reform. Since then, we have witnessed China's leaders managing her international economic policy with mounting wisdom and growing confidence. "What was striking", reported David Miliband about the recent G20 Conference, "was that when China spoke, everybody listened". Domestically, large scale state planning is certainly still evident. China's response to climate change, for example, involves major public sector investment in wind power. So too their response to the need for economic stimulus has prompted substantial public sector investment.

But Wen Jiabao emphasises that in their "socialist market economy... the market plays a *primary* role [my italics] in allocating resources under Government macro-regulation". As the leadership now strives to build a more harmonious relationship between leaders and people, this is an important part of the message – and, in my judgment, likely not just to remain so but to grow with the passage of time.

CHAPTER THIRTEEN

RESPONSIBLE CAPITALISM IN RUSSIA AND FORMER SOVIET COUNTRIES

SIR ANDREW WOOD GCMG

THIS IS A CONTENTIOUS SUBJECT. 'Responsible' and 'Capitalism' are elastic terms. Russia is a particular and changing country. Many of its neighbours have comparatively simple economies within which the state plays so dominant a role as to make it a politeness to describe them as capitalist. Others, such as Ukraine, are on a different political and societal trajectory aiming at increasing conformity to Western European business norms. The Baltic states are of course already fellow members of the European Union.

Russia, Kazakhstan, and Ukraine (especially the Eastern parts of that country), share some inherited structural characteristics that have greatly influenced their development since they became independent states. First, the sheer size of the enterprises built under the Soviet system has in all three cases been a limiting factor, along with the deep inefficiencies of many of them. Even the evidently capitalist United States has rightly or wrongly seen major enterprises as too big to fail. It is not surprising that the urge in CIS countries to preserve obsolescent, even hopeless, economic structures has been so widespread. Few would argue I think that General Motors is a worse car producer than Russia's AvtoVAZ, which has been on life support since the collapse of the Soviet Union.

Russia and Kazakhstan, like Azerbaijan, Turkmenistan and Uzbekistan, but unlike Ukraine, have, second, had the blessing or if you prefer it the curse of abundant hydrocarbon and other natural resources. Profits from these have supported state structures, encouraged monopolies rather than competition, and inhibited innovation. The average age of machinery and equipment in producing industry is 18 years. Gazprom is a notable example of a corporation that is in practice responsible in the first place to the state rather than to its wider shareholders.

And, third, all the countries of the area, and particularly Russia as the heart of the former Soviet Union, inherited an infrastructure covering basic societal needs such as transport, power generation, health, education and housing that was neither near enough to collapse to force action nor developed enough for sustained progress. Electricity generation is the only one of these that has undergone reform, in Russia, a process only just completed and whose further evolution is not yet established.

It has been argued that the chaebol system that underpinned the development of successful and vibrant capitalism in South Korea is an appropriate model for Russia to follow. But the parallel between Russia now and South Korea at the start of its transformation is strained. South Korea had been destroyed by war. Russia has been devastated by Soviet central planning, as have others in the CIS, leaving it with a substantial industrial base and a substantial managerial class that cannot simply be replaced by newly dedicated men and machinery. It is not dishonourable for many of the managers of Russia and other CIS countries today to have a rather conservative outlook, or to feel pride in what was established in Soviet times, coupled with the instinct to preserve its familiar shape. Few of them have had the chance that others like the South Koreans once had, of starting again.

In the circumstances, the achievements of the nineties were remarkable. Price liberalisation and the transfer of ownership to private hands had a measurable and stimulating effect. The times were rough and ready, but they did not deserve the reputation they have since then acquired. There was progress in the nineties, buttressed later to a useful degree by the legislative reforms of President Putin's first term towards accountability and market discipline. If the 'oligarchs' had deserved that title fewer of them would have been destroyed in 1998, and those that remained would not so easily have been cowed after President Putin took over in 2000. None of them today in Russia are more than the delegated owners of the assets they currently manage, and from which they profit.

And that of course is the difficulty in judging how far capitalists in Russia and in countries with similar polities can be deemed to be acting responsibly, within the meaning of the terms as we use them in the UK. Those in sectors regarded by the state as being 'strategic' are as responsible to the state as they are to the market. Because property rights are uncertain, and were shown to be so in 2003 with the arrest and subsequent imprisonment of Khodorkovsky, current owners' horizons are short rather than long term. Prime Minister Putin can deal with a local difficulty by instructing the owner to take up his pen and sign an agreement which he might under normal business circumstances have felt unjustified. The 'oligarch' Deripaska was acting as a functionary, not as an independent businessman when he signed up to Putin's recent demand, before the TV cameras in Pikalyovo, that he settle with restive employees.

The Financial Times described in a leader of 14th April 2009 the main features of a liberal market economy as being uncontested – "private property rights, smart but even-handed and arms-length regulation, and democratic politics." None of the CIS countries has these in adequate measure, although Georgia and Ukraine have more of them than most. All of these countries, in part because these institutional pillars are lacking, and in part because the press is muzzled and non-governmental organisations are curbed, suffer from corruption: Russia's ranking by Transparency International (147th out of 180 in 2008) is shameful, and so is Ukraine's. Corruption and Responsible Capitalism do not go together.

RESPONSIBLE CAPITALISM

Nor does Responsible Capitalism flourish in states which lack the institutional structures of a genuine constitutional system underpinned by independent courts of law.

But will things change? They may in Ukraine, which has the benefit of a rambunctious press and competitive politics. But the omens are less good elsewhere. President Medvedev declared in the run up to his election in 2008 that his main goals were developing the rule of law, and rooting out corruption. He described the four 'I's that he intended to pursue: innovation; investment; infrastructure; and institutions. All four have a bearing on the conditions under which responsible capitalism can better flourish. The results, a year on and even allowing for the global economic crisis which has hit Russia particularly hard, and for the fighting around Georgia, have yet to be evident. It is depressing that Khodorkovsky is on trial again.

The next Russian Presidential elections (this time for a six-year term instead of the four that has previously been the constitutional norm) are due in 2012. That gives little time, unless events force it, for deep-seated change. Experts from the Institute for Contemporary Development, a think tank assembled for Medvedev when he was a candidate for the Presidency similar to the one which had under Gref's guidance advised candidate Putin in 1999, revisited its 2007 analysis in the Spring of 2009. Of the four possible trajectories for Russia's development described two years ago, one ('Rentier', meaning Russia living off energy super profits) was seen this year as no longer practicable. The second ('Inertia', with the country accounting stability as preferable to development and using its reserves to deal with problems piecemeal) could work in the group's view for now but not for much longer. The third ('Mobilisation' presupposing the redistribution of assets in favour of the state) seemed to fit the current mood of the Administration since it involved centrally determined priority sectors, a leading role for state corporations, and business working to bureaucratically selected targets. Businesses could find themselves punished for social irresponsibility, as defined by officials. The state would set itself up as the guardian against market excesses, and attract public support in that role. But once started, the experts believed, it was hard to see where 'mobilisation' would stop.

The Institute's preferred course was still, as it had been in 2007, the fourth option, 'Modernisation'. This would involve the encouragement and deepening of competition through structural reform, the government setting conditions rather than directing the market: better courts, improved infrastructure, educational reforms, and so on. By common consent, however, such deep changes are for now at least improbable. As an astute member of the Duma put it in June, the authorities are concentrating on defending the old castle, not constructing a new town to live in after the present crisis is over. Not even the banking system, for all the strains it has undergone, has been significantly reformed: instead, the role of the state-related banks has grown. That would on the face of it mean 'mobilisation' not 'modernisation'.

And yet – three of them.

First, by the time this book comes out, the strains on Russia may have returned. A conservative budget directed at social protection, including job protection, may look unexciting yet credible with oil around US$70 a barrel. Things would look very different if the price started to go down again, particularly given the hit that has already happened to consumption in Russia's export markets, and the decline in Russian production too. It is not evident that the domestic credit crisis will have eased by the autumn, and liquidity is a serious problem for Russian business now, already. There will be a peak in commercial debt to foreign lenders to be surmounted in August/September, higher than the one the country faced during the first phase of its crisis.

Second, even if Russia turns out to have reached bottom, or something like it, in the middle of this year, its recovery is likely to prove 'L' shaped while the comforting assumption of the authorities is that it will rebound into familiar growth resting primarily on natural resources once again. But a repeat of the fat years of the Putin Presidency looks unlikely.

And third, there is debate going on as to where Russia is headed, and business is not complacent. The state corporations which have been set up in the last couple of years have yet to prove themselves. 'Russian Technologies' for example is a consumer of special privileges, and state money too — it is also a refuge for bankrupt enterprises. Gazprom's inefficiencies have been exposed over the past year. The state machinery in Russia is no better than it has been, making the chances of it proving an effective promoter of change extraordinarily remote. The result could be a build up of trouble leading to pressure for change.

I recall being asked a few years ago whether I would care to suggest a Russian candidate for the Responsible Capitalism award, or a nominee from one of the other CIS countries. I decided that I could not. My grounds were not so much that I could not think of businessmen in formerly Soviet countries who were behaving well in the conditions that they found themselves having to operate in, as that those conditions were too foreign to the sorts of standards likely to carry conviction with the FIRST jury. There have however been changes since then, some of them slower than one might wish, but cumulative in their effect. Accounting standards have improved. Some Boards are better than they were. Foreign investment has been beneficial both because Russian (and other CIS) firms have had to become more accountable in order to attract it, and because direct foreign investment has helped to introduce ethical know how as well as new technology. There are unsung Russian as well as foreign heroes here. And while the growth of small and medium sized enterprises in Russia and elsewhere in the CIS has been far slower than it ought to have been, there are such enterprises, some of them clear in their standards.

I therefore hope that for all the present difficulties for would-be responsible capitalists in ex-Soviet countries, the changes that are remarkable when one compares what the case is now and what it was as the Soviet Union collapsed will under the pressure of events and the interests of the peoples of the region encourage the gradual development of a true market system. If only their governments would let them...

CHAPTER FOURTEEN

RESPONSIBLE CAPITALISM IN INDIA

RATAN TATA

COMPANIES ANCHORED in poor countries like India have historically had to share additional societal responsibilities not expected of their counterparts in the West. Pioneer Indian industrialists like Jamsetji Tata, GD Birla, Jamnalal Bajaj, Lala Shri Ram, Ambalal Sarabhai and others were acutely aware of their social responsibilities. More recent developments in the Indian economy, which have enlarged the role of business, and the imperatives of global climate change have added a fresh set of social challenges for Indian companies to address. The upshot is that even though Indian companies have sought over time to become increasingly more socially responsible, a wide gap still exists between Indian society's valid expectations from business and business' track record in meeting those expectations.

Modern Indian business was nurtured in the country's independence movement and thus came of age deeply conscious of its social responsibilities. The founder of one of India's foremost business groups and one of the nation's first industrialists considered the labour of establishing his group as secondary to his mission of contributing to the industrialisation of India. He saw disciplines such as medicine and science and industries such as energy and steel as building blocks in the emergence of a bright new country. Thus, he committed the group to enter the steel and power businesses and donated 50% of his personal fortune to creating India's first institute of higher learning, the Indian Institute of Science.

Many of his contemporaries also fostered the growth of nationalism by setting up trusts and endowments to host modern institutions such as schools, colleges, hospitals, orphanages and widows' homes. Their activism was built upon by the next generation of industrialists who worked closely with Mahatma Gandhi and were influenced by his concept of business being trustees of social wealth. Two business leaders in the early decades of the 20th century pioneered a series of firsts in labour welfare practices at their plant in the Tata Iron and Steel Company which were in advance of most units in the industrialised countries too. These included: 8-hour working day (1912), free medical aid (1915), schooling facilities for children (1917), leave with pay and a provident fund scheme (1920), maternity benefit (1928), profit-sharing bonus (1928) and retiring gratuity (1937).

As India moved towards achieving independence, the nation looked to industry to partner the government in hastening economic progress. Industry responded with an act of statesmanship with the putting together by the country's leading industrialists of the Bombay Plan, India's maiden attempt at charting a planned pathway of growth. The Bombay Plan advocated sharply increasing the country's industrial growth rate as the nation's top priority and conceded a leading role for the state in seeking to achieve that objective since private industry did not possess resources in the scale the nation required. In the same spirit of nation-building, leading industrialists set up many of the nation's finest institutions of science and research like the Birla Institute of Technology, the Delhi School of Economics, Tata Institute of Fundamental Research, the Tata Institute of Social

Sciences and the Tata Memorial Hospital (the nation's first cancer hospital and research centre). Industrialists were also among the early public advocates of making family planning central to any strategy for faster economic growth.

The sixties and seventies saw the Indian state sharply increase its role in the economy, amid a growing suspicion of private industry and an increasingly higher tax regime. This led to a corresponding decrease in private philanthropy but, ironically, though perhaps not surprisingly, an increase in the setting up of 'charitable' trusts for purposes of tax planning. Industry's contribution to the national drive to eradicate smallpox in India was, however, a notable achievement of selfless corporate social responsibility in this period.

The improvement in the economic environment following the opening up of the economy, which began in 1980 and picked up pace after the 1991 reforms freeing industry from many of its shackles, proceeded to redefine many of the tenets of corporate social responsibility for Indian business. With greater global scrutiny of their operations, more Indian companies began to realise that social responsibilities come under a holistic canopy and that there was no single element of it that was more important than any other. The environment was important and responsible business could not sacrifice sustainability at the altar of profits. Similarly, doing the right thing in matters of corporate governance was as critical as maintaining good relations with employees and enriching the wider community.

Indian companies have long been expected to make a direct contribution to addressing the poor quality of nutrition, medical facilities, housing, sanitation and education available to a majority of Indians through support for agencies working in the areas of livelihood, education, health and the like. The rapid growth of the civil sector in the past few decades meant companies had to learn to work with NGOs as part of a more participatory approach to working with communities and to move from supply-driven giving to demand-led strategies.

In this period, new philanthropic leadership also came from entrepreneurs from the Information Technology industry who had benefited considerably from India's greater integration with the global value chain. These entrepreneurs gave a fillip to corporate initiatives in education, health and rural upliftment, with one eponymous foundation single-mindedly focusing on achieving "quality universal education" through improving the quality of primary education at government-run schools, mostly in the rural areas.

The agenda for improvement for Indian businesses' social responsibility, however, remains vast. The main development challenge in India remains in the villages where 70% of India still lives, and the task is too vast and too urgent to be adequately addressed by any single agency, be it the Government, the voluntary sector or the corporate sector. Only a partnership among all three will begin to address the challenge and Indian industry needs to encourage this partnership by pro-actively embracing its role in development.

The Government has finally begun to recognise the need for public private partnerships to improve the delivery of public services like education and health. The country's farm economy is in dire need of better technological inputs, agricultural extension practices and market linkages to overcome its low productivity trap. The Indian Government has sought to provide stability of rural income through the National Rural Employment Guarantee Scheme assuring employment of at least 100 days at minimum wages but the quality of the implementation of the scheme has varied with the level of local motivation, awareness and mobilisation. Local self-government has been sought to be strengthened through nation-wide elections to local bodies (called panchayats) but the degree of empowerment of local self-governance bodies is largely feeble and the management skill sets available at the grassroots to take on the development challenge is minimal. Industry needs to regard all these improvement areas as management challenges which can begin to be addressed by sharing its expertise and resources with the government and the civil sector.

The opening up of India's economy post 1991 has greatly improved the economy's growth rate but has also widened disparities. Urban areas with better aggregations of skill-sets and connectivity than rural areas have benefited disproportionately from globalisation. The more developed states have seen superior investment flows than the less developed ones and the disparity between them has grown. Poor governance and widening disparities are the main reasons why a large swathe of underdeveloped areas in the centre of India are under the spell of extremist ideologies advocating Maoist class war.

Industry needs to address the widening disparity by locating more green-field investments in the investment-starved states. Attempts to do so by Indian companies have often been thwarted by the tricky and controversial issue of land acquisition and of providing a sustainable alternative stream of occupation and income to those who only know how to till the land. Industry needs to play its part in working out an equitable consensus on both these issues through a dialogue with government and voluntary organisations representing the people affected.

Industry also has a critical role to play if India is to reap the "demographic dividend" from having the largest population of people in the productive 15-59 age group over the next few decades. For the dividend not to become a nightmare, India needs to vastly increase its supply of personnel skilled in the trades and technologies of tomorrow. India's structure of vocational training and higher education needs to be made of global standards and the numbers scaled several multitudes. The Indian government is finally beginning to concede a key role for the private sector in this key national priority and Indian industry needs to come forth with big plans to forge a partnership with the government.

Further, Indian companies need to challenge their best human resources to harness the latest in technology and business models to develop products and services which involve the larger base of the social pyramid both as a market as well as a production base. Too much of Indian industry is still focused on the urban elite. We need many more inexpensive and simple business models at the grassroots like Amul (which started off as a cooperative of milk producers from rural Gujarat and is today India's biggest foods brand) to embed sustained income creation where people live, and many more products like Professor Ashok Jhunjhunwala's corDECT (a fixed wireless local loop standard which enables reasonably robust telecommunications connectivity from sparse rural areas because of its extremely low capital costs) to harness the latest in technology for the benefit of the poor. Water should be a priority focus area for industry to develop low-cost, green technology to address the growing distress in the provision of drinking water.

The Indian Government's pursuit of inclusive growth has seen it recently asking business to go in for affirmative action in creating jobs and appointing business associates to favour the 25% of the population who are Dalits (Scheduled Castes) and tribals. Some sections of Indian industry have responded positively to the government with plans to upgrade the skill sets of these socially discriminated sections. However, what would truly jump-start the process of bringing these sections of the people into the economic mainstream would be if industry were to voluntarily set quotas for outsourcing goods and services required by their companies to firms owned by members of those communities.

Two final points in conclusion. The first is about climate change. India has been slow off the block in addressing its growing carbon emissions and Indian companies have much catching up to do in reducing their carbon footprint by adopting environment-friendly technologies.

The final point is about corruption. India's economic growth has unfortunately been accompanied by an erosion of values and ethics and Indian business has played not a small part in this deterioration. Consequently, we are in the unfortunate situation today of increasingly seeing corrupt corporations being feted for their 'social achievements'. Indian industry needs to adopt a voluntary code of ethics to eschew cartelisation and non-competitive behaviour like compromising public officials.

A point related to corruption is about ostentation. Even as one out of four Indians still lives in grinding poverty, many in the Indian corporate world lavish excessive remuneration on themselves as promoters and senior managers and indulge in the most conspicuous of consumption. This callous behaviour has besmirched the image of Indian industry. Eschewing ostentation also needs to be in the voluntary code of ethics that Indian industry needs to adopt.

The people of India look to business to play a leadership role in addressing India's most pressing social and economic challenges. Business can do this only if it keeps the nation's long-term interest uppermost at all times. India's development challenge demands nothing less.

APPENDIX

PROFILE OF THE AWARD

FIRST INSTITUTED THE AWARD for Responsible Capitalism to mark the Millennium. In making the Award, the judges are looking for a business leader who has demonstrated social responsibility as an integral part of commercial success; someone who has run a company in a clearly responsible way. What has commended the recipients to the judges has been their concern for the environment and the local communities in which their companies and organisations are active.

APPENDIX

FIRST AWARD JUDGING PANEL

THE RT HON THE Lord Woolf of Barnes (Chairman)
THE RT HON THE Lord Howe of Aberavon CH QC
HE Chief Emeka Anyaoku GCVO TC CFR
Lord Plant of Highfield
Lord Marshall of Knightsbridge, Chairman, Pirelli UK
Marilyn Carlson Nelson, Chair, Carlson Companies
Sir Robert Wilson KCMG, Chairman, BG
Dr Daniel Vasella, Chairman and Chief Executive, Novartis
Morris Tabaksblat KBE
Hon Philip Lader, Chairman, WPP Group
Ratan Tata, Chairman, Tata Sons
Sir Patrick Cormack, FSA MP
Howard Schultz, Chairman, Starbucks Coffee Company
Philippa Foster Back OBE, Director, Institute of Business Ethics

Rupert Goodman, Chairman, FIRST

APPENDIX

AWARD WINNERS AND PRESENTERS

2000 WINNER
Lord Browne of Madingley, Group Chief Executive, BP
presented by THE RT HON Gordon Brown MP,
Chancellor of the Exchequer

2001 WINNER
Marilyn Carlson Nelson, Chair and CEO, Carlson Companies
presented by THE RT HON Jack Straw MP,
Secretary of State for Foreign and Commonwealth Affairs

2002 WINNER
Sir Robert Wilson KCMG, Executive Chairman, Rio Tinto
presented by THE RT HON Patricia Hewitt MP,
Secretary of State for Trade and Industry

2003 WINNER
Dr Daniel Vasella, Chairman and CEO, Novartis, AG
presented by THE MOST REV AND THE RT HON Dr Rowan Williams,
Archbishop of Canterbury

2004 WINNERS
Morris Tabaksblat KBE, Chairman, Reed Elsevier
presented by THE RT HON THE Lord Woolf of Barnes,
Lord Chief Justice of England and Wales

Jaime Zobel de Ayala, Chairman, Ayala Group
presented by THE RT HON Lord Howe of Aberavon CH QC

APPENDIX

AWARD WINNERS AND PRESENTERS *continued*

2005 WINNER
Alan Wood CBE, Chief Executive, Siemens PLC
presented by General Sir Mike Jackson GCB CBE DSO ADC GEN,
Chief of the General Staff

2006 WINNER
Ratan Tata, Chairman, Tata Sons, the holding company of Tata Group
presented by HRH The Princess Royal

2007 WINNERS
Howard Schultz, Chairman, Starbucks Coffee Company
Thomas J. Bata, Chairman, Bata Shoe Foundation
presented by THE RT HON Alistair Darling MP,
Chancellor of the Exchequer

2008 WINNERS
Dr Mohamed Ibrahim, Founder, Celtel International,
Sir Sigmund Sternberg and Lord Dahrendorf KBE
presented by THE RT HON David Miliband MP,
Secretary of State for Foreign and Commonwealth Affairs

2009 WINNERS
Andrew Witty, Chief Executive Officer, GlaxoSmithKline
Roger Sant, Chairman, The Summit Foundation
Karim Khoja, Chief Executive Officer, Roshan Telecom
presented by George Osborne MP,
Shadow Chancellor of the Exchequer

APPENDIX

TESTIMONIALS

"Please accept my very best wishes and support for the FIRST Responsible Capitalism initiative"
HE *Pascal Lamy*
Director General, WTO

—

"Best wishes for the success of The FIRST Awards"
HE *Ban Ki-Moon*
Secretary General, United Nations

—

"The Commonwealth has a long association with FIRST and very much appreciates the opportunity to assist with the Awards"
HE *Kamalesh Sharma*
Secretary General, Commonwealth

APPENDIX

ABOUT FIRST

FIRST IS A MULTIDISCIPLINARY INTERNATIONAL AFFAIRS ORGANISATION. It aims to enhance communications between leaders in industry, finance and government, worldwide and promote strategic dialogue. This is achieved via three key channels; publishing, events and awards. The chairman of the FIRST Advisory Council is THE RT HON Lord Hurd of Westwell CH CBE.

Publishing
The recipient of a PPA Award for Publishing Excellence, FIRST Magazine is read by the world's leadership community and comprises interviews conducted with government and business leaders focusing on long term strategic issues. In addition, a comprehensive range of sectoral and regional reports and text books are produced often in co-operation with governments and leading organisations. Specialist sector specific publications include *World Petroleum* and *Global Energy*.

Event Management
FIRST organises and manages a range of high level meetings and special events for governments and corporations, ranging from conferences through round table gatherings to individual meetings between business and government leaders. Attendees include the Chairmen and CEOs of some of the world's major companies, leading academics and government ministers.

APPENDIX

ABOUT FIRST *continued*

Award Schemes
In 2000 FIRST instituted the Award for Responsible Capitalism to honour business leaders who have excelled in both commercial success and social responsibility. The adjudicating panel is chaired by THE RT HON THE Lord Woolf of Barnes and includes THE RT HON THE Lord Howe of Aberavon CH QC, HON Philip Lader, Lord Plant of Highfield, Chief Emeka Anyaoku GCVO TC CFR, Sir Patrick Cormack FSA MP, Marilyn Carlson Nelson (Chair of the Carlson Group), Sir Robert Wilson KCMG (Chairman of BG), Dr Daniel Vasella, (Chief Executive of Novartis), Morris Tabaksblat KBE, (former Chairman Reed Elsevier), Ratan Tata (Chairman of Tata Sons), Howard Schultz (Chairman, Starbucks Coffee Company) and Philipa Foster Back OBE.

INDEX

Africa, 58, 67, 70
African Governance, index of, 53
Afro-Marxists, 69
AIDS, 65
All China Federation of Trade Unions, 78
America, 55
Amul, 91
Anglo-Saxon, 55
Anglo-American economic model, 55
Anglo-Saxon economic models, 56
Anyaoku, Chief Emeka GCVO TC CFR, 4, 7, 9, 67
A Theory of the Moral Sentiments, 27
AvtoVAZ, 82
Azerbaijan, 82
Bajaj, Jamnalal, 87
Beijing Olympics, 37
Berlin Wall, 67
BG Group, 44
Birla, G. D., 87
Birla Institute of Technology, 88

Blair, THE RT HON Tony Blair, 2
Bombay Plan, 88
Brooks, David, 36
Brown, RT HON Gordon Brown MP, 7
Browne, Lord Browne of Madingley, 7
Bulgakov, Sergei, 22
Burnham, James, 29
Cabrera, Angel, 38
Cadburys, 29
Calvinist Christianity, 28
Cambridge, 76
Cameron, THE RT HON David Cameron MP, 2
Canterbury, Archbishop of, 7, 19, 25
Capitalism, 17
CARLSON, 40
Carlson, Curt, 41
Celtel International, 49-52
China, 22-23, 37, 61, 75, 77-78
China's Environmental Protection Agency, 79
Christian, 25

INDEX

Church, 25
Collectivism, 37
Common morality, 37
Commonwealth, 62-63, 65-66
Commonwealth Business, Council, 65
Commonwealth Business Council Guidelines for Corporate Citizenship, 65
Commonwealth Heads of Government, 65
Commonwealth Youth Credit Initiative, 64
Conflict diamonds, 72
Congo-Brazzaville, 49, 50
Copenhagen, 79
Cormack, Sir Patrick Cormack FSA MP, 5, 17
Corporate responsibility, 47
Corporate Social Responsibility (CSR), 52, 79
Dahrendorf, Lord Dahrendorf of Clare Market KBE FBA, 1, 3, 4, 5-7, 8-9, 11-12, 14-15, 17, 40-41
Dalits, 92
Declaration of Interdependence, 37
Delhi School of Economics, 88
Democratic Republic of the Congo, 50
Deng, Xiaoping 75, 80
Deripaska, Oleg, 83
Development assistance, 70

Doha Round, 66
Duma, 85
Dunning, John, 19
Economic rational man, 21
Enquiry into the Causes of the Wealth of Nations, 27, 68
Ericsson, 51
Ethical economy, 24
Ethical growth, 23
Ethics, 21, 38
EU, 77
Europe, 55
Extractive Industries Transparency Initiative, 63
ExxonMobil, 39
Fan Gang, 79
Financial Times, The, 73, 83
FIRST Magazine, 5, 7, 9, 11-12, 14, 16-17, 33, 40-41
Fombrun, Charles, 36
Fukuyama, Francis, 28
G20, 24, 80
Gandhi, Mahatma, 88
Gazprom, 82
General Motors, 81
Georgia, 83
Ghana, 63, 65
Goodman, Rupert, 5-7, 17, 25, 41
Governor of the Bank of England, 46
Gref, German, 84
Gujarat, 91

INDEX

Handy, Charles, 58
Harmonious society, 37
Harvard Business School, 11, 38
Homo economicus, 22
Howe, RT HON Lord Howe of Aberavon CH QC, 7, 8, 75
Ibrahim, Dr Mohamed, 49
Ideology and Development in Africa, 69
ILO, 78
India, 22, 61, 90
Indian Institute of Science, 88
Institute for Contemporary Development, 84
International Herald Tribune, 37
Jhunjhunwala, Professor Ashok, 91
Judaeo Christian, 28
Kazakhstan, 81-82
Keynes, Lord, 32
Khodorkovsky, Mikhail, 83-84
Labour Contract Law, 78
Lebedoff, David, 36
London Business School, 51
Making Globalization Good, 19
Managing revolution, 29
Maoist class war, 91
Marks & Spencer, 47
Marlborough House, 17
Marx, Karl, 28, 61
McKinnon, THE RT HON Sir Donald McKinnon, 4
Medvedev, Dmitry, 84

Miliband, RT HON David Miliband MP, 80
Millennium Development Goals, 52
Moral indifference, p.20
Morality, 31
Moral responsibility, 32
Mozambique, 65
Myners, Lord 32
National Rural Employment Guarantee Scheme, 90
Nelson, Marilyn Carlson, 9, 35
New York Times, 36
New Zealand, 63
Nigeria, 52, 63
Novartis, 58
Obama, Barack, 2
Obama administration, 56
Oligarchs, 83
Open door policy, 75
Otobo, Ejeviome Eloho, 73
Owens, Robert, 6
Panchayats, 90
Pan Yue, 79
Philanthropy, 47, 48
Pikalyovo, 83
Plant, Lord Plant of Highfield, 7-8, 27
Polanyi, Karl, 28
Putin, Vladimir, 83, 85
Responsible capitalism, 35, 37, 45, 49, 56, 64, 76
Rio Tinto, 44

INDEX

Rowntrees, 29
Russia, 81-82, 84
Russian Orthodox, 22
Rwanda, 16
Sachs, Jeffrey, 56
Saïd Business School/Oxford University, 39
Salts, Titus, 6
Sarabhai, Ambalal, 87
Schultz, Howard, 16
Schumpeter, 28
Second World War, 56
Seitz, Hon. Raymond, 7
Shanghai, 23
Shared morality, 36
Sharma, His Excellency, Kamalesh, 4, 9, 61
Shri Ram, Lala, 87
Sichuan Earthquake, 79
Siemens, 51
Sierra Leone, 49
Singapore, 63
Singh, Manmohan, 2
Smith, Adam, 27, 68
Social capital, 31
Social good, 21
South Korea, 82
Soviet Union, 82
St Antony's College, Oxford, 5, 9
Starbucks Coffee Company, 16
Stern School of Business/New York University, 36
Sternberg, Sir Sigmund, 17

Sustainable development, 47
Tabaksblat, Morris, 14
Tanzania, 65
Tata Institute of Fundamental Research, 88
Tata Iron and Steel Company, 88
Tata Memorial Hospital, 88
Tata, Jamsetji, 87
Tata, Ratan, 8, 15, 87
The Observer Newspaper Magazine, 16
The Philosophy of Economy, 22
The Princess Royal, Her Royal Highness, Princess Anne, 7, 17
The Protestant Ethic and the Spirit of Capitalism, 28
The Reputation Institute, 36
The Thunderbird School of Global Management, 38
Time Magazine, 39
Transparency International, 83
Turkmenistan, 82
UK, 77
Ukraine, 81, 83-84
Ulster, 77
United Nations (UN), 49
United Nations Global Compact, 39
Uzbekistan, 82
Vasella, Dr Daniel, 8, 55
Waitrose, 47
Wall Street, 61
Weber, Max, 28

INDEX

Wen, Jiabao, 76, 78-80
Williams, THE MOST REV AND THE RT HON Dr Rowan Williams FBA, 19, 25
Wilson, Sir Robert Wilson KCMG, 8, 43
Wood, Sir Andrew Wood GCMG, 8, 81
Woolf, THE RT HON THE Lord Woolf of Barnes, 4, 7, 14, 15
World Bank, 63, 76
World Health Organisation (WHO), 57
WTO, 24
Young, Crawford, 69
Zobel de Ayala, Jaime, 14